LEADERSHIP BASICS

Be Better Today Than You Were Yesterday

JON DOOLEN
GETDOOLEN.COM

Leadership Basics

Copyright © 2024 by Jon Doolen

All rights reserved.

No part of this book may be reproduced, distributed, or transmitted in any form or by any means, including photocopying, recording, or other electronic or mechanical methods, without the prior written permission of the publisher, except in the case of brief quotations embodied in critical reviews and certain other noncommercial uses permitted by copyright law.

For permission requests, write to the publisher at jon@getdoolen.com

Published by Doolen Strategy Partners

ISBN: 979-8-9921982-0-1

Jon Doolen

Leadership Basics

Thank you!

Jon Doolen

Leadership Basics

Acknowledgements

Gratitude, integrity, and loyalty, these three values have defined not only the journey of writing this book but the life I've been fortunate enough to live alongside some incredible people.

To my wife, **Rachael**: Thank you for being my unwavering foundation. Your love, honesty, and relentless support have carried me through a life that may not have followed a set plan but has always been guided by intention. Through every twist and turn, your faith in me and in us has been the compass that helps me rise and grow. Together, we've faced challenges and emerged stronger, proving that we can always be better today than we were yesterday. You are not just my partner in life, but my partner in purpose.

To my daughters, **Ayla and Zahra**: You are my reason, my light, and my daily reminder of the beauty in growth. Watching you explore the world with curiosity and courage has inspired me to dig deeper, to leave something behind that matters. This book is, in many ways, for you, a piece of my heart and mind, written so you can always carry a part of my journey as you carve your own. You remind me that true legacy is not in what we achieve, but in the love, lessons, and values we pass on.

To all of you: Thank you for believing in me when I doubted myself and for being the reason I continue to strive for integrity in my actions and loyalty in my commitments. You have given me more than I could ever express, and for that, I

Jon Doolen

Leadership Basics

am eternally grateful. This book is as much yours as it is mine.

In no specific order but all critically important to my growth, accountability, and development:

Allan Hoffman, Kevin Phillips, Oakland McCulloch, Mike Chanat, this book exists because of the advice guidance and feedback you gave along the way as you read my writing over the last 3 years and provided real world feedback to make it better, to make me a better storyteller.

Mike Dinitto, my consistent podcast partner in crime, for challenging my ideas and opinions and making me a better interviewer.

Dr. L. Sue Williams – you showed me that I had a story to tell, you'll notice that this book is not that story. That story has been written and will be published soon. This book is my life's professional work.

Gregg Tate, Mike Brown, Burton Oxford, your support, encouragement and honesty in my Leadership journey at critical times has been unmatched.

Patrick Cory, Scott Baker, you have been the older brothers I always wanted. You gave tough love and direct feedback when needed and encouragement to chase my goals. To this day – you're my second & third text or phone call when I am at a crossroads (my wife will always be my first).

Jon Doolen

Leadership Basics

Ellen Voie, I have been privileged to fly with many celebrities over the years, but you were the first that made me turn into a fan. Your work in the industry and your voice for women everywhere inspires me and makes me pay attention. I have not done enough yet, but because of your friendship, I will keep pushing.

Phil McLaughlin, James Donoho, Karen Rossignol, Anthony Oxtal you shared your life lessons with me and helped me be a better Leader because you showed me what real life looked like outside of the textbook.

Ron Blumkin, there is not much about my life and success today that I cannot credit you with influencing or causing. You have been the single greatest influence in me wanting to be a trainer, mentor and coach and I have been blessed to learn from you. Your family has always treated me like family and I will always try to pay it forward.

Dan Izadorak, Rick Catron, Jagdip Joshi, my current chapter has been greatly influenced by your support and your example of what it takes to build a business.

Marc Harris, Chris Jones, Brad Green each of you added in ways I am proud and grateful, you taught me how to be a better Leader and you had my full attention at critical times of growth.

Trevor Martin – watching your relentless drive is inspiring and motivating. Keep Moving Forward my friend.

Jon Doolen

Leadership Basics

Jordan Schwarz, thank you for teaching me how to self-publish on Amazon and buy ISBN's, oh and running the Detroit Half-Marathon with us – I am grateful my friend.

Each of you have played a major role in helping me become who I am, and there are probably plenty I have left off this list.

To all of my business partners, I won't name you because you know how I feel about confidentiality.

Thank you for the opportunity and trust you place in me. I think we learn as much from each other every day and I very much enjoy every moment of our time together. You allow me to serve your organization and in return you provide for my family. Thank you.

Together we are building sustainable Leadership Development programs that future generations will be proud of and grateful for.

If you have ever stopped me to tell me how much my content inspired, motivates or hits you just right, just when you needed it to hit, I am grateful for that feedback and it is literally the only fuel I need to keep pushing forward.

Some have told me they cannot connect with me on social media or follow my content because their company watches their activity and my message is threatening to weak leaders.

Jon Doolen

Leadership Basics

If that is you – please just know I see you and I will keep creating and sharing for you.

For all those who are not worried about your boss judging you, don't be afraid to Like, Follow, Share and Comment… it really does help spread the word and you never know when your digital trail helps another find their way home.

To the authors who have come before me and influenced my thinking; John C. Maxwell, Susan Cain, Simon Sinek, Liz Wiseman, Jim Collins, Rosabeth Moss Kanter, Patrick Lencioni, Herminia Ibarra, Stephen R. Covey, Brené Brown, Ken Blanchard, Sally Helgesen, Peter Drucker, Lolly Daskal, Marshall Goldsmith, Frances Frei, L. David Marquet, Kirstin Ferguson, Tony Robbins, Carol S. Dweck, James Clear, Angela Duckworth, Ryan Holiday, Robin Sharma, Dale Carnegie, Marie Forleo, Eckhart Tolle, Gabrielle Bernstein, Mark Manson, Oprah Winfrey, Daniel Goleman, Sheryl Sandberg, Mel Robbins, Rachel Hollis, and many others.

These authors and many – many more have contributed significantly to discussions on leadership, personal growth, and the tools needed to navigate and excel in both personal and professional realms.

Jon Doolen

Leadership Basics

Table of Contents

Introduction

Chapter 1: Traditional Leadership Styles and Theories

Chapter 2: Moving Beyond Traditional Leadership Theories

Chapter 3: Understanding Human Behavior

Chapter 4: Emotional Intelligence

Chapter 5: Adaptive Leadership

Chapter 6: Communication in a Real-World Context

Chapter 7: Building Trust and Credibility

Chapter 8: Leading Diverse Teams

Chapter 9: Conflict Resolution and Negotiation

Chapter 10: Building and Sustaining Relationships

Chapter 11: Leading Through Change and Crisis

Chapter 12: Continuous Learning and Development

Chapter 13: Practical Tips and Tools

Jon Doolen

Leadership Basics

Chapter 14: Let's discuss the role faith plays in Leadership

Chapter 15: The Future of Leadership

Conclusion: Reflecting on Key Themes and Final Thoughts

Citations

Jon Doolen

Leadership Basics

Introduction

As I work on the final edits of this book before publishing, I find myself asking two questions, who is Jon Doolen and why would people want to read a book he wrote about Leadership?

As I contemplated the answer to both, I was taken back to a memory of a conversation with a friend mentioned in the acknowledgements, as we discussed the various Leadership books written and how they all kind of blend together after a while.

What sets the books apart is the author's journey through leadership and the journey you are on. There are authors I click with because they speak to the experiences I have had, or they have walked a path I am on.

This book may speak to you in a way that others may not. This book may also seem like total BS to you and a rip off of what others have done in the past.

I respect that.

Leadership and some of the core principles have not changed since the Bible was first written.

We all have our own interpretation on how leadership should work and this book is intended to be a user manual for you, I tried to leave space for you to add notes as you see fit.

Jon Doolen

Leadership Basics

I also tried to stay true to the option of this book not being chronological and you can refer to the chapters as you need them. With so many other options and authors who have already written so much about the subject, why does my voice matter?

When I googled myself, I learned that I am a seasoned (old) logistics and operations executive with decades of experience in the retail, final mile home delivery, supply chain, and e-commerce sectors.

My first book idea was a Leadership manual for those in final mile as there really are not many "how to" guides for the people that bring your big and bulky items to your house.

That book turned into the training platform attached to **getdoolen.com**

I served in the U.S. Army's Quartermaster Corps (Logistics) with the 1st Infantry Division, 1st Engineer Battalion, which is not a great leadership story. I challenged authority and made life difficult for my Leadership team. I have not 'always' had an issue with taking orders, only during a time of my life when refusal to do so could have sent me to prison. (I did not go to prison, but I did mop many floors and wash lots of dishes – and did more push-ups than I can remember)

Luckily for me I had many very understanding Senior NCO's and Officers who saw where I could go. Many of them tried to get me to act right through discipline, mentorship and

Leadership Basics

friendship. I wasted a great opportunity, and that motivates me to make connections with younger generations and show them a more positive direction.

I now lead my own company, Doolen Strategy Partners, specializing in leadership development, career coaching, and personal mentorship. Previously, I have worked for some very big and successful companies owned by some of the most successful people you would recognize if I dropped their names here, and I have worked for some struggling companies and poor leaders.

Google is correct, I do have an extensive background in leadership and operations management, combined with my commitment to continuous improvement and adaptability, I hope you find after reading this that it does make my insights valuable for those seeking practical guidance in real-world leadership scenarios.

People often ask me how I achieved the success I have over the years. For me it's simple. I speak directly to the issues, and I focus on respecting the people involved.

There is another reason why this book should matter to you and your team. Over the years I have had many mentors and great leaders. Some of which have never met each other and don't know each other. They all have something similar in common. They saw the value I brought to teams, and offered this advice to other leaders they knew who were struggling…

"Get Doolen"

Jon Doolen

Leadership Basics

The first time it happened, I was visited by a leader from a different division of our company that became one of my strongest advocates, a great mentor and friend. He knows who he is. In fact – in future books there may be more than one chapter written about him.

He was reaching out because he saw the value I could add if I had the right influences guiding me toward the right goals. I did not trust him at first and even had doubts about his leadership ability, not because of anything he did, but because other leaders – jealous of his success and style, spoke badly of him when he was not present.

He taught me not to listen to the critics and stay focused on my mission. Later he would advise people who needed to solve complex problems, they needed to **Get Doolen.** He would tell them they needed my help to see the problem from different perspectives.

Over the years this same advice has been given by people who know me, my style, my success and some of my losses. They know that I can add value to almost any situation, which is how my business has taken off. My clients from a variety of industries saw value in adding me to the conversation because they decided to **Get Doolen.**

This book represents my vision and interpretation of Real-World Leadership, shaped by my experiences in the workplace outside of any formal leadership training or classrooms. It is written to help leaders navigate the inevitable challenges and obstacles they will face in their

Leadership Basics

career journeys. Much of the content is defining what leadership is and concepts that were never explained to me as I entered leadership. Where possible you will find **"Leadership Tips"** based on real-life situations that either didn't unfold the way textbook leadership principles suggested they would or just my advice for things to go better.

In the early stages of my career, when I faced unexpected reactions, I often didn't handle them well. I lacked proper training, guidance, and mentorship that truly reflected how the world operates.

Like many others, when I was promoted, there was no user manual for leading real people, just textbook assignments and classroom lessons.

One of the first times, I "had my cage rattled" came very early in my Leadership career. I had recently taken over a team of call center agents, did not have much experience representing policy or procedure and probably did not even know what the policies were.

I got called to the front counter to go face to face with a customer who had been giving the "business" to a very experienced agent who was doing her job, but the outcome the customer wanted required someone to overrule company policy.

With very little training, and probably even less experience, I did the wrong thing.

Jon Doolen

Leadership Basics

I took the side of the agent and stood my ground. The customer unleashed her verbal assault on me and let me have it. Fortunately for me, the Director's office was within ear shot and they came to my development.

Yes, you read that right. The Director did not come to my rescue, my aid or to attack me.

I was relieved of service to this customer and asked to step aside, the Director listened to the customer, supported the decisions of myself and the agent as following procedure, but The Director took the side of the customer and made the transaction happen.

Later that day I got called to the Directors office to recap what happened.

The Director started the conversation with "so, you got your cage rattled for the first time..." and then I was led down the path of self-reflection and improvement. This was a moment that could have been handled poorly and led me down a different path. It is a moment I look back on with gratitude that it was handled with dignity and compassion.

This book will explore how real-world leadership often diverges from what is taught in schools and popular leadership books. I will discuss the importance of adaptability and emotional intelligence (EI), how to process unexpected reactions, and how to build effective relationships.

Jon Doolen

Leadership Basics

The list of famous leadership writers is long, and I respect many of them. You'll notice their influence here, I've tried to avoid overused examples. Through 30 years of leadership and management, one truth stands out: humans will never act or react exactly how you expect them to. That's why it's essential to constantly evolve your knowledge and experiences. I am a strong advocate for continuing education and self-improvement.

Before I go any further, it's important to make clear, there is only one person responsible for your development.

It's you. Not your company, not your mentor or coach.

YOU must take ownership to be better today than you were yesterday.

Every leadership situation is unique. While situations may have similarities, there are always details that make them specific to you and your company. There is no one-size-fits-all solution. I encourage you to reach out to me, whether you're reading this book, listening to the audio version, or reflecting on the content.

We can discuss the methods I present, debate approaches, or talk through your challenges.

I am not hard to find!

getdoolen.com

Jon Doolen

Leadership Basics

Chapter 1: Traditional Leadership Styles and Theories

In this chapter we introduce and explore traditional leadership styles, autocratic, democratic, and laissez-faire, each offer distinct methods for guiding teams, with unique strengths and limitations. While these approaches can be effective in certain scenarios, their real-world application often reveals challenges, especially in dynamic or evolving environments.

Understanding these limitations is key for leaders, enabling them to adapt their strategies based on the specific needs of the team, task, and context. This chapter explores the core principles behind these leadership styles, highlighting their advantages and drawbacks to help leaders navigate and refine their approach in different situations.

The distinction between leadership style and leadership theory lies in their focus and purpose within the realm of leadership. Leadership style refers to the specific manner in which a leader chooses to lead, encompassing behaviors, attitudes, and approaches they employ to influence others. It's essentially about the practical execution of leadership in action.

On the other hand, leadership theory delves into the underlying principles, motivations, and ideologies that drive different leadership styles. It seeks to explain the reasons and philosophies behind effective leadership practices,

Jon Doolen

aiming to provide frameworks and models to understand and improve leadership effectiveness.

In essence, while leadership style is about the 'how' of leadership in practice, leadership theory explores the 'why' behind those practices, offering insights into what makes leadership effective and adaptable across various contexts.

Traditional Leadership Styles

Traditional leadership styles like autocratic, democratic, and laissez-faire offer distinct approaches.

Each leadership style has unique strengths but also notable limitations when applied in real-world settings. Understanding these limitations helps leaders adapt their approach based on the team, task, and environment.

Autocratic Leadership

The leader makes all decisions unilaterally, with little input from others. (Citation 14)

Autocratic leadership, can be effective in certain situations, but it also has significant limitations when applied in the real world:

Lack of Employee Engagement and Motivation: In an autocratic environment, employees often feel disconnected and disengaged because they don't have a voice in decision-making. Over time, this can lead to a lack of ownership, reduced morale, and decreased job satisfaction, ultimately impacting productivity.

Limited Innovation and Creativity: Autocratic leaders typically make decisions without consulting their team members, which stifles creativity and innovation. When employees aren't encouraged to contribute their ideas, the organization may miss out on valuable insights and new approaches to problem-solving.

Increased Turnover and Retention Issues: The top-down approach of autocratic leadership can lead to high employee turnover, especially if the work environment feels stifling or overly controlled. Talented employees may leave for companies that offer more autonomy and opportunities for personal growth.

Dependence on the Leader: An autocratic style places heavy reliance on the leader for direction and decision-making. This can create bottlenecks and slow down progress, as the team waits for the leader to make all the decisions. In the long run, it may also undermine the development of leadership skills among team members.

Communication Breakdown: Autocratic leaders often make decisions in isolation, which can lead to poor communication within the team. When decisions are not shared or explained, it creates confusion and frustration among employees who may feel left out of the process.

Leadership Basics

Risk of Poor Decision-Making: Since autocratic leaders often make decisions alone, they may not have access to diverse perspectives or the necessary expertise from team members. This can lead to flawed decision-making, especially in complex or rapidly changing situations where multiple viewpoints are important.

Resistance to Change: Autocratic leadership tends to resist feedback, especially if it challenges the leader's authority. This can prevent the organization from adapting to new trends, technologies, or market shifts, which is crucial in today's fast-paced business environment.

Toxic Work Environment: If taken to an extreme, autocratic leadership can foster a toxic work environment marked by fear, resentment, and low morale. Employees may feel powerless or even hostile toward the leader, which undermines collaboration and teamwork.

In summary, while autocratic leadership can be effective in crisis situations or where clear direction is needed, its limitations make it less suitable for organizations that thrive on collaboration, creativity, and employee development.

Democratic Leadership

Involves seeking input from team members before making decisions. (Citation 15)

Leadership Basics

While democratic leadership can promote collaboration and innovation, it also has limitations in certain real-world situations:

Slow Decision-Making: One of the most common criticisms of democratic leadership is that it can lead to slow decision-making. Involving multiple people in the decision-making process can result in lengthy discussions and delays, particularly when a decision needs to be made quickly or during a crisis.

Difficulty in Reaching Consensus: In a democratic system, where input from everyone is valued, it can sometimes be difficult to reach a consensus. When team members have conflicting views, the decision-making process can become prolonged, and the final decision may not satisfy everyone, leading to dissatisfaction or indecision.

Risk of Confusion and Lack of Direction: While collaboration can be beneficial, too much involvement in decision-making may result in a lack of clear direction. If the team has too much input or if the leader doesn't provide strong guidance, the group may struggle to move forward or set priorities, leading to confusion or inaction.

Leadership Strain and Overload: In a democratic leadership model, the leader must facilitate open discussions, gather feedback, and ensure all voices are heard, which can become time-consuming and taxing. The leader may also feel pressure to align decisions with the team's preferences, rather than making tough calls that could be unpopular but necessary.

Potential for Groupthink: While democratic leadership encourages diverse opinions, it can sometimes lead to groupthink, especially if the leader pushes for consensus too hard. In such cases, team members might suppress their true opinions to avoid conflict or align with the majority, which can stifle critical thinking and creativity.

Challenges in Accountability: Democratic leadership often involves shared responsibility, which can sometimes make it unclear who is accountable for specific decisions. In situations where accountability is crucial, such as when things go wrong, it may be difficult to pinpoint the individual or group responsible for a failure.

Inconsistent Decision Quality: The quality of decisions may vary depending on the level of expertise or experience of the individuals involved. A leader may want to involve everyone in the decision-making process, but not all team members have the same level of knowledge or insight, which can lead to suboptimal decisions or missed opportunities.

Employee Overload or Confusion in Priorities: When every decision is subject to group input, employees may feel overwhelmed with the number of decisions they are asked to weigh in on. This can also create confusion about priorities, especially if there's a lack of clarity regarding which decisions require collaborative input and which ones are better left to the leader.

Leadership Basics

Difficulty Managing Conflicts: In a democratic environment, disagreements can arise when team members have differing views. While healthy debate is encouraged, unresolved conflicts or continual disagreements can cause friction and hinder progress, making it hard to maintain harmony and productivity within the team.

Leader's Role Can Be Diluted: A leader in a democratic environment may find their role diluted as the focus shifts to group consensus. In situations requiring clear and decisive leadership, the leader may struggle to assert authority or provide direction, which could weaken their influence or the effectiveness of the team.

In summary, while democratic leadership can foster collaboration, innovation, and engagement, its limitations—particularly in decision-making speed, accountability, and managing conflict—can make it challenging in environments where quick, clear decisions and strong leadership are needed. It works best in settings where team members are capable, and the decision-making process is more complex or creative in nature.

Laissez-faire Leadership

A hands-off approach where the leader gives autonomy to team members. This works best with highly skilled, self-motivated teams but can lead to confusion or lack of direction without proper guidance. (Citation 16)

Leadership Basics

Laissez-faire leadership, characterized by minimal direct intervention and allowing team members the freedom to make their own decisions, can be effective in some environments, especially with highly skilled, self-motivated teams.

However, it has notable limitations in real-world applications:

Lack of Direction: One of the primary criticisms of laissez-faire leadership is that it can lead to a lack of clear direction. With little guidance or oversight, team members might struggle to understand the overall vision or goals, leading to confusion and misalignment. Without a clear framework or leadership structure, projects can go off track.

Inconsistent Accountability: When a leader takes a hands-off approach, it can be difficult to hold individuals accountable for their actions. If the team members are given freedom without clear oversight, it may lead to some team members neglecting their responsibilities, or others taking on too much, creating an imbalance in workload and accountability.

Reduced Team Cohesion: In laissez-faire leadership, the leader's minimal involvement can lead to weak team cohesion. Without regular guidance, communication, and support from the leader, team members may feel disconnected from each other or from the larger organizational goals. This can hinder collaboration and create silos within the team.

Potential for Low Productivity: While some employees thrive under minimal supervision, others may struggle without clear structure. In a laissez-faire environment, employees who need more guidance or motivation may become disengaged, leading to low productivity and inefficiency.

Without constant direction, some individuals may not fully utilize their potential or take proactive steps to reach their goals.

Lack of Development and Feedback: Without regular leadership involvement, team members may not receive the guidance, feedback, or development they need to improve. Continuous learning and improvement require active support and mentorship from leaders. If a leader isn't actively engaging with team members, they may miss opportunities to offer constructive feedback and help individuals grow.

Difficulty in Crisis Situations: Laissez-faire leadership can be particularly ineffective in crisis situations. When urgent decisions need to be made or when rapid responses are required, a lack of leadership intervention can slow down the team's response.

In such scenarios, a more direct approach from a leader is often necessary to guide the team and make swift, informed decisions.

Leadership Basics

Limited Innovation and Risk-Taking: In laissez-faire leadership, the lack of structured guidance and proactive leadership may stifle innovation and risk-taking. Without a leader pushing boundaries or encouraging new ideas, team members might stick to familiar methods and avoid experimenting with more creative or disruptive solutions.

The absence of a guiding hand can sometimes result in a lack of initiative or willingness to innovate.

Potential for Confusion About Roles: In a laissez-faire environment, the ambiguity about roles and responsibilities can lead to confusion among team members.

Without clear direction from the leader, team members may be uncertain about their specific duties or the boundaries of their responsibilities. This can create misunderstandings, overlapping duties, or tasks being neglected altogether.

Ineffective Leadership in Developing Teams: Laissez-faire leadership assumes that employees are already self-motivated and capable of managing their own work. However, this may not be the case in many teams, particularly with less experienced or newer team members.

Without active mentorship or guidance from the leader, there's limited opportunity to develop team members' skills and potential.

Difficulty Managing Conflicts: Conflict resolution may be neglected in a laissez-faire setting. Since the leader is less

Leadership Basics

involved in day-to-day operations, unresolved conflicts between team members can escalate without intervention.

A lack of leadership input can make it difficult to mediate disputes, leading to a toxic work environment or decreased morale among employees.

Decreased Leader Influence
A hands-off approach can reduce the leader's influence within the team. In a workplace where leadership is detached or passive, employees may lose respect for the leader, perceiving them as uninvolved or uninterested in the team's success.

This erosion of authority can undermine the leader's effectiveness, particularly when guidance or decision-making is needed.

Over-reliance on Self-Motivated Individuals
Laissez-faire leadership works best with highly self-motivated and skilled individuals, but not all employees are at that level. When a team is not composed of self-starters, a lack of direction and support can lead to under-performance or missed opportunities. Leaders may inadvertently place too much responsibility on individuals who aren't yet capable of working independently without clear guidance.

In summary, while laissez-faire leadership can be effective in certain contexts, such as with autonomous, experienced teams, it has notable limitations in environments requiring clear direction, structure, and accountability.

Without active leadership involvement, there is a risk of confusion, low productivity, and disengagement, especially when team members lack the skills, motivation, or guidance needed to thrive independently.

Traditional Leadership Theories

Now I will explore five leadership theories: Trait, Behavioral, Contingency, Transformational and Servant Leadership. They offer valuable frameworks for understanding leadership principles, focusing on qualities, behaviors, and situational adaptability.

Trait Theory: Focuses on identifying qualities like intelligence, decisiveness, and integrity that make someone a leader. (Citation 1)

Leadership Tip: Assess your own traits and identify areas for growth. Seek feedback from trusted colleagues to gain insight into your natural strengths and blind spots.

Behavioral Theory: Emphasizes the behaviors that effective leaders exhibit, such as being task-oriented or relationship-oriented. (Citation 2)

Leadership Tip: Observe and adapt your behaviors to suit the needs of your team. Balance task-oriented and relationship-oriented approaches.

Leadership Basics

Contingency Theory: Suggests that effective leadership depends on the situation, requiring different styles based on specific circumstances. (Citation 3)

Leadership Tip: Evaluate your current leadership style and consider whether it fits the situation. Be prepared to adjust your approach.

Transformational Leadership Theory: Focuses on inspiring and motivating followers by setting clear goals and communicating a vision. (Citation 4)

Leadership Tip: Communicate your vision clearly and set achievable, inspiring goals to keep your team aligned and motivated.

Servant Leadership Theory: Focuses on serving others first, prioritizing the growth and well-being of individuals and the community. (Citation 5)

Leadership Tip: Prioritize listening and empowering your team members to build trust and drive growth.

These traditional theories are all useful in understanding leadership, but they provide static frameworks that may not adapt well to modern, evolving organizations.

They fall short when applied to the unpredictable and dynamic challenges of modern organizations. The need for contextual intelligence - adapting leadership strategies based on cultural, environmental, and situational factors - has become increasingly apparent.

Conclusion

Traditional leadership styles, autocratic, democratic, and laissez-faire, each offer valuable insights into leadership, but none are universally perfect. While they provide foundational strategies for guiding teams, their limitations become evident when applied in real-world, ever-changing contexts.

Autocratic leadership can drive quick decisions but stifles creativity and engagement. Democratic leadership fosters collaboration but may slow decision-making. Laissez-faire leadership offers autonomy but risks lack of direction and accountability.

To thrive in today's complex environments, leaders must move beyond rigid adherence to any single style and instead adopt a flexible, situational approach. The ability to assess the needs of the team, the task at hand, and the broader organizational environment is crucial.

By recognizing the strengths and weaknesses of these traditional approaches, leaders can refine their strategies, creating a more adaptive, responsive, and effective leadership style that fosters both individual and collective success.

Chapter 2: Moving Beyond Traditional Leadership Theories

Leadership requires more than just textbook knowledge. The real world demands flexibility, emotional intelligence, and contextual awareness. To thrive, leaders must be adaptable, intuitive, and willing to evolve as situations change.

By acknowledging the limitations of traditional theories and continuously learning, leaders can effectively navigate the complexities of modern organizations.

Traditional leadership theories provide foundational knowledge, but fall short in addressing the complexities of the real world

These theories are widely respected and have practical applications, but they were primarily developed through controlled studies and ideal scenarios. They do not account for the nuances and variability encountered in everyday leadership and the unpredictability of human reactions.

Factors Influencing Human Behavior

Humans react differently based on various factors, including:

Economics: Individuals who place a high value on financial success will react differently than those who don't. People caught up in financial status are usually easy to spot in a crowd but be careful. This is one of the easiest to fake, most people are swimming in debt just to look like they have more than you.

Leadership Basics

Placing a high value on wealth or financial success is, in my opinion, focusing on the wrong things. Making money is great, and I hope you make as much as you need, but don't lose sight of your goals. Money can make people do things and react to situations under duress.

Influence: People who are influenced by social factors will act differently depending on how they perceive their position relative to others. If someone feels disrespected or a loss of credibility due to a situation they will react outside of their normal character.

In some cases, they may have a "second thought" reaction to a situation and show some regret for their initial response but social status can play a bigger role than financial status in some cases.

I witnessed someone almost have a medical event when they felt they were being attacked in a Facebook post, they demanded the person who wrote it and posted it take it down and post a retraction. I could not understand why they put so much value on the online opinion of others.

Power Status: Reactions often vary depending on the perceived organizational status of the individuals involved. People who feel their authority, status or standing within an organization, even if its only perceived status being threatened can react in very toxic ways, sometimes very passive aggressive.

The mere fear of having some power or authority taken can be

Leadership Basics

enough to set someone off and cause a reaction outside of how they would normally process information.

I once worked with a guy so hungry for position and authority that he would turn from a polite, warm and friendly leader to an aggressive bully if he felt his position was being threatened.

He was almost unrecognizable when it was in full lash out mode, but I learned how to recognize when it was happening in the starting stages and either feed his ego to avoid being the target or just get out of his line of sight.

His wrath knew no limits, he would target peers and sometimes superiors. His tenure did not last long and over the course of the last 20 years he has left a path of broken relationships, both personally and professionally.

Leadership Tip: Remember that leadership is about people, not just theories. Build relationships, foster trust, and adapt to the ever-changing human element of your organization.

Contextual Intelligence

Traditional theories often overlook the importance of **contextual intelligence**, which is the ability to adapt leadership approaches based on specific situations.

Contextual intelligence involves understanding the dynamics of a given situation, such as culture, values, and external factors, and

Leadership Basics

responding appropriately to achieve the best outcomes. Leaders who demonstrate this ability can adjust their strategies based on team dynamics, market conditions, and organizational culture. (Citation 6)

For example, the rewards and leadership strategies used when leading a call center are different and not as effective in a blue-collar warehouse. The stress instigators are different and the way each person handles and processes their stress is unique.

A customer service agent getting yelled at for something they had no control over generally requires an emotional reset that won't look the same as the warehouse worker who just stripped their fourth set of headboard bolts.

Here are some examples highlighting how rewards and leadership strategies that are effective in a blue-collar warehouse might not directly translate to leading a call center:

Incentives and Motivation

- **Warehouse**: Physical tasks are often rewarded with tangible incentives like gift cards for high output, bonuses for exceeding quotas, or recognition for safe practices.

- **Call Center**: Workers are typically motivated by recognition for emotional labor and problem-solving. Incentives might need to include emotional support, such as awards for customer satisfaction or

Leadership Basics

programs that reduce stress from handling difficult customers.

Leadership Style

- **Warehouse**: Leaders often use a hands-on, directive approach. Tasks are clear and outcomes are measured physically (e.g., number of packages moved).

- **Call Center**: Leaders must focus on emotional intelligence and coaching, as tasks are more nuanced. Emphasis on communication skills and conflict resolution is critical when dealing with varied customer interactions.

Performance Metrics

- **Warehouse**: Success is often measured quantitatively, such as the speed and accuracy of tasks.

- **Call Center**: Performance is measured qualitatively as well as quantitatively, such as customer satisfaction scores, resolution time, and empathy displayed during calls.

Leadership Basics

Team Dynamics

- **Warehouse**: Collaboration may involve clear, physical workflows, such as passing items down an assembly line.

- **Call Center**: Teamwork is less tangible and may involve sharing best practices, mentoring, or covering shifts for others while managing one's own queue.

Stress Management

- **Warehouse**: Stress is often physical, related to meeting quotas or avoiding injuries, so strategies like breaks and ergonomic tools are effective.

- **Call Center**: Stress is emotional, often stemming from handling unhappy customers. Leadership might focus on mental health resources, team-building activities, or flexible scheduling.

Recognition

- **Warehouse**: Recognition might center on physical achievement or endurance, like awards for highest output or attendance.

- **Call Center**: Recognition should highlight soft skills, like handling a tough customer with grace or providing exceptional service during a high-stress period.

Work Environment

- **Warehouse**: Leaders often focus on creating a safe and efficient physical space, ensuring proper equipment and layout.

- **Call Center**: Leaders must prioritize a positive emotional environment, ensuring morale stays high through communication, supportive management, and incentives that address mental fatigue.

Different work environments, risk factors, and emotional responses demand individualized leadership approaches. Stress management strategies should be tailored to the nature of the work. Leaders must adapt their style to meet the distinct needs of each environment.

Leadership Tip: Take time to understand the unique dynamics of your team and work environment. Regularly solicit input to align your leadership strategies with the context.

Contingency Theory versus Contextual Theory

There are so many factors that can influence how someone will react to a situation, the same person can react to the exact same stimuli differently depending on what they are currently dealing with at the time.

Leadership Basics

Factors such as financial stress, faith, health, perceived threats, hunger or fatigue.

The difference between contingency theory and contextual theory lies in the focus and approach by the leader. Both theories emphasize adaptability, but the approach is from slightly different angles.

Contingency Theory

- **Focus**: Matching leadership style to the situation.
- **Key Idea**: There is no single best way to lead; effectiveness depends on the fit between the leader's traits/behavior and situational variables.
- **Emphasis**:
    - Leader's style (e.g., task-oriented or relationship-oriented).
    - Situational factors (e.g., leader-member relations, task structure, position power).
    - Leadership effectiveness changes based on altering **situational conditions**.
- **Example**: A task-oriented leader might thrive in a structured, high-control environment, whereas a relationship-oriented leader might excel in a low-control, ambiguous situation.
- **Prominent Model**: Fiedler's Contingency Model.

Leadership Tip: Identify the situational factors influencing your team, such as task structure or interpersonal relationships, and tailor your leadership approach accordingly.

Jon Doolen

Leadership Basics

Contextual Theory

- **Focus**: Leadership influenced by broader environmental, cultural, and social factors.

- **Key Idea**: Leadership and organizational effectiveness are shaped by the **context**, including external forces, organizational culture, and situational dynamics.

- **Emphasis**:
    - **External environment** (e.g., market conditions, technology, cultural norms).
    - **Internal dynamics** (e.g., organizational culture, team dynamics, historical influences).
    - Leadership strategies evolve based on **understanding and adapting to the context** holistically.

- **Example**: A leader in a startup may adopt a flexible, innovative approach due to the dynamic industry context, while a leader in a traditional industry might focus on stability and consistency.

Leadership Tip: Study the broader cultural and environmental factors impacting your team. Adapt your strategies to address both internal and external influences.

Leadership Basics

Key Differences

Aspect	Contingency Theory	Contextual Theory
Core Question	How does leadership style align with situational factors?	How do environmental and cultural contexts shape leadership?
Scope	Focused on immediate, situational factors.	Broader focus on environmental and systemic influences.
Leadership Adaptation	Based on internal leader-situation fit.	Based on external and internal environmental demands.
Perspective	Situation-specific, tactical.	Holistic, strategic.

In short, **contingency theory** is more about tailoring leadership to specific, defined situations, while **contextual theory** considers a broader, more holistic perspective on how external and internal contexts shape leadership.

The Role of Practical Experience and Intuition

One-size-fits-all solutions are no longer effective. Traditional theories may oversimplify human behavior and fail to address the irrationality and emotional complexity of individuals. Leaders must adapt their strategies based on real-time feedback and the emotional states of their teams.

For example, during organizational change, employees may fear many things, including additional workload. Trust and empathy become crucial in managing such transitions.

In crises, such as staffing shortages, unplanned spikes in workload or more serious matters like natural disasters or financial downturns, rigid adherence to traditional leadership theories can be detrimental. Effective crisis management requires adaptive decision-making and clear communication.

Jon Doolen

Leadership Basics

Leadership Tip: In times of crisis, focus on clear communication and emotional support. Maintain transparency and involve your team in problem-solving.

Practical experience is essential for developing intuition, which enables leaders to make quick, informed decisions in complex situations. Intuition, often honed through experience, helps leaders navigate crises and adapt to unforeseen challenges.

Leadership Tip: Reflect on past experiences to develop intuition. Keep a journal of challenges faced, decisions made, and lessons learned to build a personal leadership toolkit.

Conclusion

Human behavior is influenced by a variety of factors, from economic pressures and social dynamics to power status and environmental context. Leaders must recognize that these influences shape how individuals react, especially in moments of stress or perceived threats. Whether it's financial stress, the need for social recognition, or the fear of losing power, each factor plays a role in determining behavior.

Effective leadership requires flexibility. Theories like contingency and contextual leadership highlight the importance of adapting to the specific situation, environment, and team dynamics. A leader who

Leadership Basics

understands these nuances can foster trust, motivate employees, and navigate challenges with empathy.

Leaders who draw on practical experience and intuition are better equipped to make quick, informed decisions during crises or transitions. Recognizing the unique needs of individuals in different roles, whether in a call center or a warehouse, ensures that leadership strategies are effective and impactful.

Ultimately, leadership isn't about following a set of rigid rules but about building relationships, understanding context, and adjusting approaches to meet the evolving needs of both the team and the organization. By staying adaptable, compassionate, and focused on people, leaders can guide their teams through both everyday challenges and unexpected crises.

Jon Doolen

Leadership Basics

Chapter 3: Understanding Human Behavior

In this chapter, we will explore why human behavior is intricate, unpredictable, and shaped by a myriad of influences, including emotions, societal norms, personal experiences, and cognitive biases.

While traditional leadership models provide valuable foundational frameworks, they often fall short in addressing the irrational and dynamic nature of human decision-making.

Effective leadership today requires a deeper understanding of these behavioral complexities and the ability to adapt to evolving contexts. By integrating principles of behavioral economics, a field that combines psychology and economics to explore how people make decisions, leaders can better manage team dynamics, foster collaboration, and guide individuals toward positive outcomes.

This chapter explores key behavioral concepts, the limitations of traditional leadership theories, and practical strategies leaders can apply to navigate the emotional, social, and cognitive drivers of human behavior in real-world scenarios.

The Complexity of Human Behavior

Human behavior is often unpredictable and influenced by various factors, such as personal experiences, emotions, societal norms, and cognitive biases. Traditional leadership models, which often assume rational decision-making, fall short when addressing this complexity.

To be effective, leaders need to understand the underlying drivers of human behavior and apply insights from behavioral economics to navigate these challenges.

Behavioral economics is a field of study that combines insights from psychology and economics to understand how people make decisions. Unlike traditional economics, which assumes people are always logical and make decisions that are best for them, behavioral economics acknowledges that people often make decisions based on biases, emotions, social influences, and other psychological factors that deviate from rational behavior. (Citation 7)

Key concepts:

- **Heuristics**: Mental shortcuts or rules of thumb that people use to make decisions quickly, but which can sometimes lead to errors or biases.

- **Framing effect**: The way information is presented can influence how people perceive it and make decisions.

Leadership Basics

- **Loss aversion**: People tend to prefer avoiding losses over acquiring equivalent gains, making them more sensitive to potential losses than to gains of the same size.

- **Endowment effect**: People tend to value things they own more highly than things they do not, simply because they own them.

- **Nudging**: Using subtle interventions or changes in how choices are presented to influence people's decisions in a predictable way, without restricting their freedom of choice.

Behavioral economics helps explain why people sometimes make decisions that don't align with traditional economic theory, such as why they might spend impulsively, save less than they should, or act based on emotions rather than logic.

Traditional Economic Theory in Leadership refers to the application of classical economic principles to leadership and decision-making in organizations. This approach views leadership primarily through the lens of rationality, efficiency, and getting the most benefit. This assumes that individuals and organizations act in ways that maximize their resources and outcomes in a logical and predictable manner. (Citation 8)

Leadership Basics

Key Principles:

- **Rational Decision-Making:** Assumes leaders make decisions based on objective data, clear goals, and logical analysis to achieve the best outcomes for the organization.

- **Profit Maximization:** Leadership is guided by the idea that the ultimate goal is to maximize profits or outputs while minimizing costs.

- **Incentives and Motivation:** Traditional economic theory suggests that individuals are primarily motivated by financial incentives, such as pay, bonuses, and other material rewards.

- **Hierarchical Structures:** Leadership is often seen as a top-down process where clear authority and control ensure efficiency and productivity.

- **Predictable Behavior:** Assumes that individuals within organizations behave predictably, responding rationally to policies, incentives, and market conditions.

Behavioral Economics and Traditional Economic Theory differ significantly in how they view human behavior, decision-making, and the assumptions they rely on.

Leadership Basics

Here's a breakdown of their key differences:

Summary

Aspect	Traditional Economic Theory	Behavioral Economics
Human Behavior	Rational, self-interested	Irrational, biased, context-driven
Decision-Making	Logical, deliberate	Influenced by emotions, heuristics
Preferences	Stable, consistent	Context-dependent, inconsistent
Motivation	Financial incentives	Financial + non-financial factors
Risk Evaluation	Objective, probability-based	Biased by emotions, availability
Policy Approach	Incentives (taxes, subsidies)	Nudges, choice architecture
Methods	Mathematical models	Psychology + experiments

Here is a more detailed comparison:

Human Behavior

- **Traditional Economic Theory**: Assumes people are rational actors who make decisions to maximize utility (benefits) and minimize costs. It is based on the idea of homo economicus (economic man), who has perfect information, unlimited cognitive capacity, and consistent preferences.

- **Behavioral Economics**: Recognizes that people are often irrational and influenced by emotions, biases, and cognitive limitations.
Decisions are shaped by heuristics (mental shortcuts), biases (like loss aversion or confirmation bias), and social factors.

Leadership Basics

Decision-Making Process

- **Traditional Economic Theory:** Assumes decisions are made through careful, logical analysis of all available information. Choices are consistent and predictable under similar circumstances.

- **Behavioral Economics:** Decisions are influenced by context, framing, and how choices are presented (e.g., nudges). People often rely on incomplete information, gut feelings, or rules of thumb.

Rationality

- **Traditional Economic Theory:** Views humans as consistently rational and self-interested, always acting in their best interest.

- **Behavioral Economics:** Highlights bounded rationality, meaning people have limited cognitive resources and are often inconsistent in their preferences and decision-making.

View of Preferences

- **Traditional Economic Theory:** Assumes preferences are stable, consistent, and unaffected by external influences.

- **Behavioral Economics:** Shows that preferences are context-dependent and can be manipulated by how choices are framed (e.g., loss aversion makes people dislike losing more than they like equivalent gains).

Incentives and Motivation

- **Traditional Economic Theory**: Focuses on financial and material incentives as the primary motivators.

- **Behavioral Economics**: Acknowledges the role of non-financial incentives such as fairness, altruism, social norms, and intrinsic motivations.

Risk Perception

- **Traditional Economic Theory**: Assumes individuals evaluate risks and rewards objectively using probability and expected outcomes.

- **Behavioral Economics**: Demonstrates that risk perception is biased by factors like recency, availability heuristic, and emotional impact (e.g., people fear dramatic, rare events like plane crashes more than common risks like car accidents).

Policy Implications

- **Traditional Economic Theory**: Emphasizes policies that rely on rational actors responding to incentives, such as tax changes or subsidies.

Leadership Basics

- **Behavioral Economics**: Suggests "nudges," small changes in the choice architecture (how options are presented) to encourage better decisions without restricting freedom (e.g., automatic enrollment in retirement savings plans).

Tools and Methods

- **Traditional Economic Theory**: Uses mathematical models based on assumptions of rationality and equilibrium.

- **Behavioral Economics**: Relies on psychological experiments, observational studies, and real-world data to understand behavior.

Behavioral economics essentially challenges the assumptions of traditional theory by integrating psychology into the study of economic decision-making, offering a more realistic and nuanced view of how people behave in the real world.

Critiques of Traditional Economic Theory in Leadership:

- **Ignores Human Behavior Nuances**: Traditional theory often overlooks the emotional, social, and psychological factors that drive human behavior, which are emphasized in modern approaches like behavioral economics or transformational leadership.

Leadership Basics

- **Overemphasis on Rationality**: Assumes all decisions are made logically, while in reality, biases, emotions, and imperfect information often influence leadership decisions.

- **Limited View of Motivation**: Focuses heavily on financial incentives and neglects intrinsic motivators like purpose, recognition, and personal growth.

Evolution in Leadership Thought

Traditional economic theory laid the foundation for understanding organizational efficiency and decision-making. Modern leadership frameworks now integrate insights from psychology, behavioral science, and social dynamics to address the complexities of human behavior and organizational culture.

Concepts like emotional intelligence, adaptive leadership, and contextual leadership expand beyond the purely rational and transactional approach of traditional economic theory.

The Role of Emotions in Decision-Making

Emotions play a significant role in decision-making. People's actions are often driven by how they feel, rather than logical reasoning. Emotions like fear, anger, joy, and sadness can dramatically impact choices, leading to outcomes that defy textbook expectations. Leaders must be able to recognize

Leadership Basics

the emotional drivers of the behavior or reaction to navigate these unpredictable situations.

Recognizing the emotional drivers behind behavior or reactions can be challenging, but there are strategies leaders can use to navigate these unpredictable situations effectively:

Active Listening
- Pay attention to both what is said and how it is said. Tone of voice, choice of words, and pacing can provide clues to emotional drivers.
- Avoid interrupting and ask open-ended questions like, *"Can you share more about what's on your mind?"*

Observe Non-Verbal Cues
- Look for body language signals such as crossed arms, fidgeting, or lack of eye contact.
- Facial expressions, posture, and gestures often reveal emotions that words may not.

Understand Context
- Consider external factors like stress from deadlines, personal struggles, or workplace dynamics.
- Ask yourself, *"What could be influencing this person's state of mind right now?"*

Leadership Basics

Build Psychological Safety
- Create an environment where team members feel safe expressing their emotions without fear of judgment.
- Use phrases like, *"I want to understand what you're feeling so I can support you better."*

Ask the Right Questions
- Go beyond surface-level inquiries by asking questions like:
    - *"What's been challenging for you recently?"*
    - *"How do you feel about what's happening?"*
- This can uncover the underlying emotion (e.g., fear, frustration, or anxiety).

Acknowledge and Validate Emotions
- Recognize their feelings without trying to immediately "fix" the situation.
- Say things like, *"I can see why that would make you upset."* This builds trust and opens the door for problem-solving.

Leverage Emotional Intelligence (EI)
- Practice self-awareness to recognize your own biases and triggers that may cloud judgment.
- Use empathy to put yourself in their shoes and understand their perspective.

Leadership Basics

Identify Patterns in Behavior
- Look for recurring reactions or emotional responses in similar situations. This can help you predict future reactions and address root causes.
- For example, if someone reacts defensively to feedback, it might signal a fear of criticism or failure.

Provide Space for Reflection
- Sometimes, emotions need time to settle.
- Offer space by saying, *"Take some time to process, and let's revisit this conversation when you're ready."*

Address Emotional Drivers Directly
- Once you've identified the emotion, speak to it. For example:
    - If fear is the driver, reassure them with support and resources.
    - If frustration is the issue, collaborate to find solutions and eliminate bottlenecks.

Consider Their Perspective
- Ask yourself, *"If I were in their situation, how might I feel?"*
- Understanding their point of view can guide your approach.

Practice Patience
- Emotions can be unpredictable and don't always resolve quickly.
- Show patience as the individual works through their feelings.

Social Influences on Behavior

Social norms and peer pressure heavily influence behavior. People often conform to the expectations of those around them, sometimes against their better judgment.

Understanding and recognizing how social influences affect your team allows leaders to manage these pressures and guide their team toward positive behavior.

Here's how you can achieve this:

Observe Team Dynamics
- Pay attention to how team members interact. Who are the influencers? Who tends to follow?
- Notice patterns in group behavior, such as conformity during meetings or hesitance to speak up.
- Example: If one vocal team member dominates discussions, others may feel pressured to agree, even if they have differing opinions.

Understand Group Norms
- Identify the unwritten rules and expectations within the team. These norms often shape behavior more than formal policies.
- Ask yourself: *"What behaviors are being encouraged or discouraged in this team environment?"*

Leadership Tip: Encourage norms that promote inclusivity and respect, such as active listening and valuing diverse perspectives.

Leadership Basics

Recognize Peer Pressure
- Be aware of how peer pressure might influence decisions or behaviors, both positively and negatively.
- Peer pressure can lead to innovation if channeled correctly but can also create a toxic environment if it encourages unhealthy competition or exclusion.

Leadership Tip: Create a culture where constructive feedback and individuality are valued over conformity.

Identify Social Roles
- Every team has roles such as leaders, mediators, or dissenters. Understand how these roles shape interactions and decision-making.
- Recognize if certain individuals feel marginalized or excluded due to social hierarchies.
- Example: A junior team member may hesitate to share ideas in front of more senior colleagues, limiting creativity.

Monitor the Impact of Social Media and Technology
- Social influences often extend beyond the workplace through platforms like LinkedIn or group chats. Understand how online dynamics affect your team.
- Be aware of the impact of comparison or perceived expectations on team morale.

Leadership Tip: Promote transparency and open dialogue to counter the negative effects of online pressures.

Leadership Basics

Encourage Open Communication
- Create opportunities for honest conversations about team dynamics. Use one-on-ones, surveys, or open forums to gather insights.
- Ask questions like, *"What's working well in our team dynamic? Where can we improve?"*

Leadership Tip: Address concerns about favoritism, cliques, or unfair treatment promptly to maintain trust.

Leverage Positive Social Influence
- Identify team members who consistently model positive behaviors and values, such as collaboration, empathy, or accountability.
- Empower these individuals to influence others by highlighting their contributions and encouraging mentorship.

Leadership Tip: Recognize and reward team members who support their peers or exemplify company values.

Promote Inclusion
- Ensure all voices are heard, particularly those who may feel overshadowed by stronger personalities.
- Facilitate structured discussions where everyone has a chance to contribute.

Leadership Tip: Use techniques like round-robin discussions to equalize participation in meetings.

Leadership Basics

Address Toxic Behaviors
- Social influences can lead to negative behaviors like gossip, exclusion, or passive-aggressiveness. These can quickly erode team morale.
- Confront toxic behaviors directly and reinforce expectations for mutual respect and professionalism.

Leadership Tip: Implement clear consequences for behavior that undermines team cohesion.

Foster a Strong Team Identity
- Encourage a sense of belonging by aligning the team around shared goals and values.
- Help team members see their contributions as part of a greater purpose.

Leadership Tip: Celebrate collective successes to build camaraderie and reinforce positive social connections.

Be a Role Model
- Your actions as a leader significantly influence team behavior. Model the respect, empathy, and collaboration you want to see.
- Avoid favoritism, public criticism, or other behaviors that could create social divides.

Create Psychological Safety
- When team members feel safe expressing themselves without fear of judgment or retaliation, they're less likely to succumb to negative social pressures.

Jon Doolen

Leadership Basics

- Encourage constructive debate and reassure the team that diverse opinions are valued.

Leadership Tip: Say things like, "It's okay to disagree. Let's explore all perspectives before deciding."

Cognitive Biases and Irrational Decisions

Cognitive biases are systematic patterns of deviation from rationality in judgment, which can lead to irrational decisions.

Some common biases include:

- **Confirmation Bias:** The tendency to search for and interpret information in a way that confirms preexisting beliefs. (Citation 9)

- **Anchoring Bias:** Relying too heavily on the first piece of information encountered when making decisions. (Citation 10)

- **Availability Heuristic:** Overestimating the importance of information that is most readily available. (Citation 11)

Personal experiences, personality traits, and individual values contribute to the diversity of human behavior. What motivates one person may not motivate another, so understanding these differences is crucial for effective leadership.

Leadership Basics

Insights from Behavioral Economics

Behavioral economics combines psychology and economics to explain why people sometimes make irrational decisions. Some key concepts that leaders can use to manage behavior include:

Loss Aversion: People tend to prefer avoiding losses rather than acquiring equivalent gains. This can make employees resistant to changes, even if they offer potential benefits. For example, employees may react negatively to a pay raise if they fear it will lead to more work later.

Leadership Tip: Present changes by focusing on what can be gained by adapting and the potential risks or setbacks of staying the same. Highlight how taking action can prevent challenges and secure better outcomes.

Prospect Theory: People often make decisions based on perceived gains, rather than actual outcomes. For example, employees may choose safer, less risky projects over more ambitious ones with higher rewards but also higher risks.

Leadership Tip: Present options in a way that aligns with how individuals perceive value. Highlight potential gains and provide reassurances to mitigate perceived risks.

Overconfidence Bias: People tend to overestimate their abilities and knowledge, leading to poor decision-making and taking on too much responsibility.

Jon Doolen

Leadership Basics

Leadership Tip: Encourage a culture of humility and continuous learning. Provide constructive feedback and create an environment where team members feel comfortable acknowledging their limitations.

Social Proof: People often follow the actions of others, especially in uncertain situations. This can lead to herd behavior, where individuals conform to group norms, even irrationally.

Leadership Tip: Leverage social proof by highlighting positive behaviors and successes within the team. Use testimonials, case studies, and endorsements to influence behavior positively.

Practical Leadership Examples

Motivating a Diverse Team: Recognize that different team members are motivated by different factors. Some may value recognition, while others are driven by financial incentives or opportunities for growth.

Leadership Tip: Get to know your people and tailor your motivational strategies accordingly. Implement flexible reward systems, allowing employees to choose from various incentives based on their preferences.

Managing Resistance to Change: When introducing change, expect resistance and address it proactively. Use empathetic communication to understand team members' concerns and fears.

Leadership Tip: Hold open forums or town hall meetings where employees can voice concerns. Address these concerns transparently and involve employees in the change process to increase buy-in. One-on-one meetings may be necessary for those who prefer more private discussions.

Encouraging Risk-Taking and Innovation: Create a safe environment where employees feel comfortable taking risks without fear of severe repercussions for failure.

Leadership Tip: Implement a "fail fast, learn faster" approach. Encourage small-scale experiments, share lessons learned from failures, and foster a culture of continuous improvement.

Enhancing Decision-Making: Acknowledge cognitive biases and implement strategies to mitigate their impact. Use diverse teams to provide multiple perspectives and challenge assumptions.

Leadership Tip: Appoint a "devil's advocate" during decision-making to question assumptions and provide alternative viewpoints. This can help counteract group think and improve decision quality.

Conclusion

Effective leadership in today's dynamic world requires more than an understanding of traditional theories, it demands an

Leadership Basics

appreciation of the complexities of human behavior and the factors that drive decision-making.

By integrating insights from behavioral economics and recognizing the emotional, social, and cognitive influences on behavior, leaders can navigate the unpredictability of their teams with empathy and precision.

By embracing this approach, leaders can build trust, inspire innovation, and guide their teams toward achieving meaningful and sustainable outcomes, even in the face of uncertainty.

Chapter 4: Emotional Intelligence

In this chapter, I will define emotional intelligence (EI) and its components, offer strategies for developing self-awareness, self-regulation, empathy, and social skills, and explain how these traits contribute to effective leadership.

Emotional Intelligence (EI) and Emotional Quotient (EQ) are foundational concepts that empower leaders to navigate the complexities of human behavior and foster strong, productive relationships.

While EI represents the ability to recognize, understand, and manage emotions, EQ serves as the measurable score of this skill set. Together, they enable leaders to communicate effectively, resolve conflicts, and inspire their teams.

In today's dynamic and emotionally charged workplace, EI is more critical than ever, influencing decision-making, motivation, and resilience. This chapter explores the components of EI, strategies for its development, and practical applications that underscore its importance in building trust, enhancing engagement, and driving leadership success.

Through personal reflections and actionable leadership tips, this chapter demonstrates how mastering EI can transform not only individual leadership styles but also entire teams.

Leadership Basics

Emotional Intelligence and Emotional Quotient

EI and EQ are often used interchangeably, but they have slightly different meanings and connotations.

Here's a clear breakdown of the two concepts:

EI refers to the ability to recognize, understand, and manage your own emotions while also being able to influence the emotions of others. It plays a critical role in building relationships, decision-making, and managing stress effectively. (Citation 12)

EQ is the measurable score or assessment of someone's emotional intelligence, similar to how IQ measures intellectual ability. (Citation 13)

Of the two, EI is the broader concept, encompassing actual ability and skills. A person with high EI can navigate complex emotional situations, such as resolving conflicts or building strong relationships.

EQ is the measurable representation of EI, typically assessed through tools or tests. A person with a high EQ score has demonstrated proficiency in these abilities through an assessment.

Leadership Basics

Key Differences

Aspect	Emotional Intelligence (EI)	Emotional Quotient (EQ)
Meaning	The broader ability to understand and manage emotions.	The measurable score of Emotional Intelligence.
Focus	Skills, behaviors, and understanding.	Quantification and evaluation.
Nature	Qualitative and skill-based.	Quantitative and assessment-based.
Use	Practical applications in real-world situations.	Used for benchmarking or evaluation.

Emotional intelligence, first discussed in 1990 by Peter Salovey and John Mayer, is the ability to recognize, understand, and manage our own emotions, as well as the emotions of others. EI is a crucial trait for effective leadership, enabling leaders to build strong relationships, navigate social complexities, and make informed, empathetic decisions.

Components of Emotional Intelligence

Emotional intelligence consists of five main components:

Self-Awareness: The ability to recognize and understand your own emotions, strengths, weaknesses, values, and motives. Self-awareness helps you understand how your emotions affect your thoughts and behavior and how they impact others.

Leadership Tip: Start your day by asking yourself, "What emotions am I bringing to work today?" Recognizing your emotional state sets the tone for your interactions.

Leadership Basics

Self-Regulation: The ability to manage and control your emotions, impulses, and behaviors. This involves staying composed and positive, even in stressful situations, and thinking before acting.

Leadership Tip: Before reacting to a challenging situation, take a 5-second pause to reset your thoughts and approach with clarity.

Motivation: The internal drive to achieve goals for personal reasons rather than external rewards. It involves a passion for work, persistence in the face of obstacles, and commitment to personal and organizational goals.

Leadership Tip: Set daily micro-goals to keep your focus sharp and celebrate small wins to maintain momentum.

Empathy: The ability to understand and share the feelings of others. Empathy involves recognizing and appreciating others' perspectives and emotions and responding with compassion and understanding.

Leadership Tip: Spend 5 extra minutes in conversations to fully listen and validate the other person's perspective.

Social Skills: The ability to manage relationships effectively. This includes communication, conflict resolution, influence, leadership, and teamwork.

Leadership Basics

Leadership Tip: After meetings, follow up with a quick message of appreciation or encouragement to maintain connection and trust.

Strategies for Developing Emotional Intelligence

Developing emotional intelligence is key to enhancing leadership effectiveness.

Here are some strategies to strengthen each component:

Develop Self-Awareness:

- **Practice Mindfulness**: Stop what you're doing to process how you feel and why you feel that way. Engage in mindfulness practices such as meditation, deep breathing exercises, or journaling to become more aware of your emotions and how they influence your thoughts and actions.
- **Seek Feedback**: Ask trusted colleagues, mentors, or friends for honest feedback on how they perceive your emotional responses. Reflect on this feedback to identify areas for improvement. Honest feedback does not come from people with an interest in the outcome of your mission outside of clapping for you. This means, if they gain in some way from your success or failure, that needs to play a factor in how you process their advice. Have good people in your circle and have a big circle.

Leadership Basics

- **Self-Reflection**: Regularly take time to reflect on your experiences, emotions, and reactions. Keep a journal to track emotional patterns and identify areas where improvement is needed. Often, it's not others causing your emotional reactions, but your response to them.

Leadership Tip: Schedule weekly reflection time to evaluate your emotional responses and identify triggers.

Improve Self-Regulation:

- **Manage Stress**: Develop healthy coping mechanisms for stress, such as exercise, hobbies, or relaxation techniques. Practice staying calm under pressure by pausing and reflecting before reacting to situations.

- **Set Goals**: Establish personal and professional goals. Focus on what you can control and work towards these goals with a positive mindset.

Leadership Tip: Keep a "trigger journal" to document situations that test your patience and brainstorm strategies for improvement.

Enhance Empathy:

- **Active Listening**: Practice active listening by giving your full attention to others, asking clarifying questions, and reflecting on what they say. This shows you value their perspective.

- **Observe Non-Verbal Cues**: Pay attention to body language, facial expressions, and tone of voice to understand others' emotions and feelings better. Show compassion and offer support when needed.

Leadership Tip: After a tough conversation, ask yourself, "What might this person be experiencing that I don't see?"

Improve Social Skills:

- **Build Rapport**: Take time to connect with others on a personal authentic level. Show genuine interest in their lives and experiences.

- **Develop Communication Skills**: Practice clear and effective communication, articulating your thoughts concisely, and listening actively to others.

- **Conflict Resolution**: Learn and practice conflict resolution techniques. Approach conflicts with a problem-solving mindset and aim for win-win solutions.

- **Influence and Inspire**: Share your vision and align team goals with organizational objectives to motivate and inspire others.

Leadership Basics

Leadership Tip: Practice giving constructive feedback by starting with positives, addressing concerns clearly, and ending with encouragement.

How Emotional Intelligence Contributes to Effective Leadership

EI is essential for effective leadership in several key ways:

Enhances Decision-Making: Leaders with high EI make better decisions by managing their own emotions and considering the emotional impact of their decisions on others. This leads to more balanced, thoughtful outcomes.

Leadership Tip: Before making a decision, consider how it will emotionally impact key stakeholders and adjust accordingly.

Builds Stronger Relationships: EI enables leaders to build strong, trusting relationships with team members, colleagues, and stakeholders. By understanding and responding to others' emotions, leaders foster a collaborative work environment.

Leadership Tip: Commit to one personal check-in per week with a team member to strengthen connections.

Improves Communication: Leaders with high EI can communicate clearly and empathetically, ensuring their team feels understood and valued.

Jon Doolen

Leadership Basics

Leadership Tip: Before delivering important messages, consider the perspective of your audience. Ask yourself, "How might they feel about this?" Start by acknowledging their emotions and concerns, then tailor your message to address those feelings while clearly outlining your intentions. Always follow up by inviting questions or feedback to ensure mutual understanding.

Aids in Conflict Resolution: Emotionally intelligent leaders can navigate conflicts effectively, understanding different perspectives and finding resolutions that satisfy all parties.

Leadership Tip: During conflicts, repeat the other person's concerns to ensure they feel heard before presenting solutions.

Increases Motivation and Engagement: Leaders who are emotionally intelligent inspire and motivate their teams by recognizing and addressing emotional needs, leading to higher engagement, satisfaction, and productivity.

Leadership Tip: Regularly acknowledge and celebrate individual and team achievements, no matter how small. Take time to understand what uniquely motivates each team member—whether it's recognition, growth opportunities, or meaningful work—and tailor your approach to meet those needs. Personalizing your encouragement creates a stronger emotional connection and boosts engagement.

Jon Doolen

Leadership Basics

Builds Resilience and Adaptability: EI helps leaders remain resilient and adaptable in the face of challenges. By understanding their emotions and the emotional landscape of their teams, leaders can navigate uncertainty with confidence and composure.

Leadership Tip: During challenging times, model resilience by openly acknowledging difficulties while maintaining a solution-focused mindset. Share how you manage your own emotions and uncertainties to set an example. Encourage your team to voice their concerns and work together to adapt, emphasizing flexibility and collective problem-solving as key strengths.

Trust and Collaboration: EI helps leaders build trust and foster collaboration. Empathy and effective communication strengthen relationships, and leaders with high EI can navigate conflicts tactfully, finding solutions that satisfy everyone involved.

Leadership Tip: Foster trust by consistently delivering on small promises. Reliability builds emotional capital with your team.

Why Emotional Intelligence Matters

EI is often a stronger predictor of success than IQ alone. It helps people:

- Build trust and foster better relationships.

Leadership Basics

- Communicate effectively in both personal and professional settings.
- Navigate complex social situations.
- Make balanced, thoughtful decisions under pressure.

In leadership and teamwork, EI can create a positive and collaborative environment, enabling everyone to thrive.

A Leadership Misstep: Learning the Value of Emotional Intelligence

In the early stages of the 2020 COVID outbreak, I made a leadership mistake that I'll never forget. Like many others, I was navigating uncertainty, trying to keep both myself and my team afloat during an unprecedented time. But in my effort to lead, I overlooked one critical thing, what my team was personally going through.

Back then, I assumed we were all on the same page. I thought that if I could just share how I was feeling and what I was doing to stay focused, it would resonate with everyone. Without asking, I projected my own struggles onto them. I assumed they were facing the same challenges I was, fear for their health, stress over the unknowns, and the overwhelming weight of adapting to remote work. I thought I was being relatable, but instead, I missed the mark completely.

The truth was, my team's experiences were incredibly diverse. Some were single parents juggling full-time jobs while homeschooling their kids. Others were worried about

Leadership Basics

elderly family members or struggling with isolation. Some had partners who had lost jobs, and a few even had loved ones battling the virus. They didn't need my perspective; they needed to share their own.

Instead of fostering an environment where they felt heard and understood, I had unintentionally made it all about me. My intention wasn't to be dismissive, but my actions had that effect.

I had failed to lead with emotional intelligence. I didn't take the time to ask them how they were doing or what they needed from me. Instead, I projected my reality onto theirs, assuming that my experience was universal.

That moment was a humbling wake-up call. I realized that leadership isn't about having all the answers or setting the tone based on your own perspective. It's about listening - truly listening - and understanding the unique challenges your team is facing.

From that point forward, I made a deliberate effort to change. I began scheduling one-on-one check-ins with each team member, not to talk about work, but to ask them, "How are *you* doing? What are you dealing with right now?" I learned to pause before speaking, considering their perspectives and emotions before sharing my own.

Leadership Tip: Sometimes, the best way to lead is to let your team do the talking. Ask questions. Acknowledge their feelings before diving into logistics or solutions. By

Jon Doolen

doing so, you create a space where people feel valued, respected, and safe. And when they feel that way, they're far more likely to stay engaged, productive, and loyal, even in the face of uncertainty.

It took me far too long to realize the critical role adaptability and EI play in effective leadership. I didn't truly lead well until I understood these concepts. Once I grasped them, managing my own emotions and understanding others became much easier.

A Lesson in Controlling My Ego

My journey into EI also taught me the importance of controlling my ego. I allowed my ego to stand in the way during a challenging assignment. I was working long hours for a startup 3rd Party Logistics and Freight Forwarding company, which presented its own unique leadership challenges, on top of that, the client was demanding.

A new leader was hired, that leader quickly recognized my lack of EI, which was critical to my success in the role. During our weekly leadership meetings, books on EI would come up.

At first, I resisted. My ego was too inflated, and I felt I was better than the team. As these books were discussed, I realized I couldn't contribute meaningfully.

This leader, perhaps knowing exactly how to play the situation, saw through my ego and lack of EI. They knew how

Leadership Basics

to get me to engage with the books. I dove into the content and quickly saw how relevant it was to my role and challenges.

Whether or not the leader had this exact outcome in mind or just wanted me to succeed so they could, I'll never know. What matters is that I set aside my ego and embraced EI, making a change that would shape my leadership journey.

Leadership Tip: Ask a trusted mentor or colleague to provide honest feedback on how your ego may be influencing your leadership style. Use this input to adjust and grow.

I lacked EI when I first began leading, and it's clear in the damage I caused to relationships, some beyond repair. I failed to develop EI for too long. Without it, leadership is ineffective.

Today, no matter the leadership role, EI is essential. I wish I had understood its importance earlier in my career. My lack of EI caused unnecessary anxiety during times when I thought things were out of control.

I see now that many situations were not about me at all, most people are focused on their own world and their own problems. My lack of EI prevented me from adapting quickly, making me a weak leader who was always reacting instead of staying ahead.

Jon Doolen

Conclusion

EI is not just a desirable trait; it is an essential foundation for effective leadership.

By developing self-awareness, self-regulation, empathy, motivation, and social skills, leaders can navigate the emotional complexities of their teams and foster an environment of trust, collaboration, and resilience.

The ability to understand and manage emotions - both your own and others' - is key to making better decisions, inspiring motivation, and resolving conflicts in ways that strengthen relationships.
Leaders who embrace EI are better equipped to adapt to challenges, guide their teams with confidence, and create a positive, thriving workplace culture.

As demonstrated throughout this chapter, cultivating emotional intelligence is not only transformative for leadership success but also for personal growth and meaningful connections with others.

Leadership Basics

Chapter 5: Adaptive Leadership

In this chapter, I will introduce the concept of adaptive leadership, developed by Ronald Heifetz and Marty Linsky. Adaptability and emotional intelligence (EI) are essential qualities for effective leadership.

Adaptability empowers leaders to adjust to new challenges, embrace change, and foster resilience within their teams. EI, on the other hand, enhances a leader's ability to manage emotions, build trust, and inspire collaboration.

Together, these traits create a powerful foundation for navigating uncertainty, solving complex problems, and driving innovation. Adaptive leadership emphasizes the need for flexibility, collaboration, and continuous learning, distinguishing itself from traditional leadership models by addressing the unpredictability of modern challenges.

This chapter explores the core elements of adaptability and EI, offering practical strategies and leadership tips to help leaders embrace change, engage their teams, and foster a culture of resilience and innovation.

By mastering these skills, leaders can thrive in any environment and empower their teams to do the same.

Leadership Basics

Recognizing the Importance of Adaptability

Adaptability means the ability to adjust to new conditions, challenges, or environments with flexibility and resilience. It's about being open to change, learning from new experiences, and finding ways to thrive even when circumstances are unexpected or difficult.

In practice, adaptability often includes:

- **Problem-Solving:** Finding creative solutions to new challenges.
- **Emotional Resilience:** Staying calm and focused in the face of uncertainty or setbacks.
- **Learning Agility:** Quickly acquiring and applying new skills or knowledge.
- **Openness to Feedback:** Listening, reflecting, and making improvements when needed.
- **Proactivity:** Anticipating changes and preparing for them ahead of time.

In both personal and professional life, adaptability is a valuable trait, helping individuals and teams navigate change successfully, embrace innovation, and grow from experience.

Why Adaptability Matters in Leadership

Life and leadership constantly evolve due to many factors like technological advancements, economic shifts, and regulatory changes. Adaptable leaders can pivot strategies to stay competitive.

Being adaptable means staying open to change, especially when things don't go as planned.

It involves adjusting to new situations, learning quickly, and trying different approaches. Adaptable people are often excellent problem-solvers, and businesses that embrace adaptability can remain relevant and productive despite challenges.

Adaptability requires strategic thinking and a growth mindset, viewing challenges as opportunities to learn. It's about staying prepared to evolve. Adaptable leaders manage crises, adopt new technologies to drive innovation, and create supportive environments for diverse, multigenerational teams.

Leadership Tip: Start each week by asking your team, "What's one unexpected challenge we overcame last week, and what did we learn from it?" Reflecting on adaptability reinforces its value.

What is Adaptive Leadership?

Adaptive leadership is a dynamic and flexible approach to leadership that emphasizes the ability to respond to changing environments and complex challenges. Unlike traditional leadership theories that often rely on fixed strategies and hierarchical structures, Adaptive leadership encourages innovation, continuous learning, and resilience.

Leadership Basics

It acknowledges that the modern world is unpredictable, and leaders must be versatile and open to ongoing development.

Heifetz and Linsky argue that traditional leadership often falls short in addressing "adaptive challenges" those that cannot be solved with existing knowledge or routine procedures. Adaptive leadership focuses on mobilizing people to tackle tough problems and thrive in a rapidly changing world. (Citation 14)

Leadership Tip: During team discussions, challenge your group to identify one "adaptive challenge" they are currently facing and brainstorm potential innovative solutions together.

Key Differences from Traditional Leadership Theories

Focus on Change and Adaptation: While traditional leadership models often emphasize maintaining stability within established frameworks, adaptive leadership prioritizes change and adaptation, recognizing that the ability to evolve is crucial for long-term success.

Collaborative Problem-Solving: Traditional leadership tends to rely on top-down decision-making and hierarchical authority. In contrast, adaptive leadership values collaborative problem-solving, engaging team members at all levels in the decision-making process.

Leadership Basics

Learning Orientation: Unlike traditional models that may focus heavily on established knowledge and past experiences, adaptive leadership embraces a learning orientation. It encourages continuous learning, experimentation, and the integration of new insights.

Managing Complexity: Adaptive leadership recognizes that modern challenges are complex and multifaceted. While traditional leadership may simplify problems to fit existing solutions, adaptive leadership seeks to address the root causes of challenges rather than just the symptoms.

Prioritizing Emotional Intelligence and Resilience: While traditional leadership emphasizes technical skills, adaptive leadership places a strong emphasis on emotional intelligence, resilience, and the ability to manage stress in both personal and organizational contexts.

Strategies for Becoming an Adaptive Leader

Embrace Change: Stay informed about industry trends, technological advancements, and global developments. Being aware of external changes allows you to anticipate and respond proactively.

Leadership Tip: Dedicate 10 minutes each week to reading about industry trends or attending webinars to stay informed and proactive about upcoming changes.

Leadership Basics

Cultivate Flexibility: Develop the ability to pivot and adjust strategies as circumstances evolve. Foster a culture where change is seen as an opportunity for growth rather than a threat.

Leadership Tip: In your next team meeting, ask, "What's one way we could approach this differently?" Encourage out-of-the-box thinking.

Empower Your Team: Involve your team in the change process. Seek their input, address their concerns, and make them active participants in implementing change.

Leadership Tip: Delegate responsibility for a small project to a team member, giving them ownership and confidence in navigating changes.

Learn from Failure: Promote a growth mindset within your team. Encourage calculated risks and frame setbacks as opportunities for learning. After a failure, reflect on what went wrong, NOT who was wrong, analyze the situation, and share lessons learned with your team.

Leadership Tip: After a failed initiative, host a "Lessons Learned" session. Focus the conversation on insights gained rather than assigning blame.

Foster Innovation:
- **Encourage Experimentation**: Create a safe space for team members to test new ideas without fear of

Leadership Basics

punishment. Support small-scale experiments and pilot projects.
- **Promote Diverse Thinking**: Encourage interdisciplinary collaboration and diverse perspectives, as these lead to more innovative solutions.
- **Reward Creativity**: Celebrate creative efforts and recognize innovative contributions, reinforcing the value of innovation within the organization.

Leadership Tip: Create a monthly "innovation hour" where your team can propose and discuss new ideas without judgment.

Develop Emotional Intelligence and Resilience:
- **Self-Awareness and Self-Regulation**: Encourage your team to manage their emotions effectively, not suppress them. This helps them stay composed under pressure and make better decisions.
- **Empathy and Relationship Building**: Cultivate empathy by actively listening and understanding your team's perspectives. Model this behavior to strengthen collaboration and trust within the team.
- **Stress Management**: Openly discuss stress management strategies and encourage healthy coping mechanisms such as exercise, mindfulness, and maintaining a work-life balance.

Leadership Tip: Begin team meetings with a quick mindfulness exercise or an open check-in to set a calm and connected tone.

Jon Doolen

Leadership Basics

Engaging Stakeholders

- **Transparent Communication**: Maintain open and honest communication with all stakeholders. Articulate the vision, goals, and progress, while being upfront about challenges and uncertainties.

Leadership Tip: Before presenting a new idea to stakeholders, draft a concise, honest summary that addresses both potential benefits and challenges.

- **Build Coalitions**: Form alliances with key stakeholders both within and outside the organization. These coalitions can offer support, resources, and diverse insights to strengthen your adaptive capacity.

Leadership Tip: Identify one potential ally in your organization and set up a meeting to discuss how your goals align and how you can support each other.

- **Seek Feedback**: Regularly solicit feedback from stakeholders to understand their needs and perspectives. Use this feedback to refine strategies and improve your approach.

Leadership Tip: Use a quick online survey or one-on-one chats to gather feedback from stakeholders, showing them that their input is valued and acted upon.

Conclusion

Adaptability and emotional intelligence are not just leadership buzzwords, they are essential skills for navigating the complexities of an ever-changing world. Leaders who embrace adaptability can pivot strategies, foster innovation, and empower their teams to face challenges with resilience and creativity.

Similarly, EI equips leaders to build trust, manage stress, and create meaningful connections, fostering an environment of collaboration and growth. By integrating these qualities into their leadership approach, leaders can drive sustainable success for themselves, their teams, and their organizations.

The path to becoming an adaptive, emotionally intelligent leader requires intentional practice, self-reflection, and a commitment to continuous learning—but the rewards are undeniable. With these tools, leaders can inspire confidence, navigate uncertainty, and thrive in even the most unpredictable circumstances.

Chapter 6: Communication in a Real-World Context

In this chapter, I will highlight the importance of effective communication in leadership. Effective communication lies at the heart of successful leadership. It is the foundation for building trust, fostering collaboration, and driving team alignment.

Leaders who communicate effectively inspire their teams, resolve conflicts constructively, and create an open, supportive culture that enables growth and innovation. However, communication is not just about what is said but how it is perceived. Personal biases, experiences, and perspectives can shape how messages are interpreted, making clarity and empathy essential.

This chapter delves into the critical elements of effective communication, such as active listening, providing constructive feedback, and handling difficult conversations with tact and empathy. Through practical tips and actionable strategies, it explores how leaders can refine their communication skills to build trust, engage their teams, and create a culture of openness and continuous improvement.

By mastering these skills, leaders can enhance their impact, strengthen relationships, and foster a collaborative, high-performing work environment.

Leadership Basics

The Importance of Effective Communication in Leadership

Effective communication is a cornerstone of successful leadership. It fosters understanding, builds trust, and facilitates collaboration within teams. Leaders who excel in communication can inspire and motivate their teams, resolve conflicts efficiently, and create a positive organizational culture. Without effective communication, leaders struggle to align their teams, address concerns, or inspire growth.

The biggest challenge in communication is that we often communicate in a way that makes sense to us, rather than how the audience will perceive it. We all bring biases and experiences to every conversation, which can impact how we interpret and respond to messages.

Leadership Tip: Before communicating an important message, ask yourself, "How might this be perceived by my team?" Adjust your tone and approach to ensure clarity and understanding.

Clear and transparent communication builds trust between leaders and their teams. When leaders communicate openly and honestly, it fosters mutual respect, creating an environment of trust that is essential for effective collaboration. This trust helps to align efforts, reduces misunderstandings, and enhances teamwork and productivity.

Jon Doolen

Leadership Basics

Leadership Tip: Set a weekly check-in to share updates and encourage questions. Transparency builds trust and prevents misunderstandings.

Effective communication is especially crucial during times of change. Leaders need to clearly articulate the vision, explain the reasons for change, and address any concerns. This approach helps reduce resistance and gain buy-in from the team. Moreover, conflicts are inevitable, and effective communicators can address issues before they escalate, facilitating constructive dialogue and finding mutually beneficial solutions.

Leaders who communicate well also use their skills to inspire and motivate teams. Sharing a compelling vision, recognizing achievements, and offering encouragement maintains high levels of motivation and engagement. By incorporating personal stories, leaders make themselves more relatable, helping the team build trust and understand their thought processes.

Active Listening

Active listening is a crucial leadership skill. It enables leaders to understand and respond effectively to their team members' needs and concerns.

Here are some suggestions on how to be an active listener:

Leadership Basics

Give full attention: Focus entirely on the speaker, avoiding distractions. Maintain eye contact, nod, and use facial expressions to show engagement.

Leadership Tip: In your next one-on-one or meeting, challenge yourself to focus fully on the speaker. After they finish speaking, summarize what you heard before responding. Not only does this show engagement, but it also ensures mutual understanding and strengthens your connection with your team.

Allow the speaker to finish: Don't interrupt. Listen to understand, not to respond immediately. This is hard. Control your facial expressions and take notes on what they are saying to help you remember your response points.

Leadership Tip: During conversations, jot down key points instead of formulating responses. This keeps your focus on understanding the speaker rather than planning your reply.

Summarize and ask clarifying questions to ensure understanding. Here are some examples:
- "Let me make sure I understand what you're suggesting"
- "Great. One thing I want to clarify is…"
- "Can we talk more about this…"

Leadership Tip: End conversations with a summary, such as, "Here's what I'm taking away from this discussion.

Jon Doolen

Does that sound accurate?" This ensures alignment and builds trust.

Acknowledge emotions: Respond with empathy, showing that you understand and respect the speaker's feelings. Specifically say out loud that you understand and respect their opinions, thoughts and/ or perspective, this does not mean you must agree with them and you can add that, if you feel necessary, with a simple: "While I understand and respect that, I do not agree".

Leadership Tip: If emotions run high, acknowledge feelings with statements like, "I can see this is frustrating. Let's work through it together." Empathy diffuses tension and opens dialogue.

By practicing active listening, leaders show their team that their input is valued, fostering a culture of open communication.

Providing Constructive Feedback

Feedback is essential for growth and improvement. Effective feedback should be specific, balanced, and focused on behavior rather than personality.

Here are some suggestions on how to provide constructive feedback.

Leadership Basics

Be specific:
- Provide clear examples of the behavior you're addressing. Avoid vague statements like "do better." Focus on specific incidents, explaining the context and impact.
- When giving feedback to your team, try using specific examples. It's not just about what you say, but how you say it.
- Example: When I give my daughters specific feedback on what they did well and why, I see a notable difference in their response, compared to when I give a generic "great job."

Leadership Tip: Skip generic feedback like "Good job" and instead say, "Your attention to detail in that report was impressive—it really helped clarify the main points." Specific praise fosters motivation.

Balance criticism and praise: Avoid the "feedback sandwich." It's been done and it's too predictable and insincere. Instead, focus on actionable advice and be direct. Overloading feedback with too much positive reinforcement before addressing the issue can dilute the message. People appreciate direct feedback. It does not have to be rude to be direct.

Leadership Tip: Use a "describe-impact-solution" approach: "Here's what I observed, here's how it affects the team, and here's how we can address it together." This keeps feedback actionable and collaborative.

Leadership Basics

Timely feedback: Provide feedback as soon as possible after the behavior occurs. The quicker the feedback, the more relevant and effective it will be.

Leadership Tip: Make it a habit to offer feedback within 24 hours of observing the behavior. Use the "SBI method" (Situation, Behavior, Impact): describe the situation, the specific behavior, and its impact. For example, "In yesterday's meeting (Situation), you presented clear and concise data (Behavior), which helped the team quickly make a decision (Impact)." This approach keeps feedback relevant, constructive, and actionable.

Focus on behavior, not personality: When discussing areas for improvement, target the behavior, not the individual. Use statements like, "I noticed you missed a deadline, and it's affecting the team's progress. How can I help you get this done?" This keeps the conversation constructive and non-confrontational.

Leadership Tip: If someone struggles to meet expectations, ask, "What challenges are you facing, and how can I support you?" This keeps the conversation constructive and solution-focused.

Handling Difficult Conversations with Tact and Empathy

Difficult conversations are part of leadership, whether addressing performance issues, resolving conflicts, or

Leadership Basics

delivering bad news. Handling these discussions with tact and empathy is essential to maintaining positive relationships and a supportive work environment.

Prepare ahead: Gather all relevant facts and consider possible reactions. Plan how you'll address the issue and what you hope to achieve. Always aim for a productive conversation.

Leadership Tip: Before entering a difficult conversation, rehearse key points and questions. Anticipate reactions to stay composed and effective.

Choose the right setting: Conduct difficult conversations in private, comfortable settings. This helps the person feel safe to express themselves without added pressure.

Leadership Tip: Before the conversation, find a private space, let the person know the purpose of the meeting, and set a calm, professional tone. Begin by expressing your intent to support and understand, creating an atmosphere of trust.

Ask for their perspective: Allow the individual to share their understanding of what happened. This helps determine whether they're aware of the issue or if there's an underlying reason behind their behavior.

Leadership Tip: Start difficult conversations by saying, "I'd like to understand your point of view before we

Jon Doolen

Leadership Basics

discuss a solution." This approach builds mutual respect and opens communication.

Stay calm and composed: Maintain a level head, even if the conversation becomes tense. Stay composed to prevent escalation and ensure the discussion stays focused.

Leadership Tip: Practice controlled breathing before and during tense conversations. If emotions rise, pause briefly to collect your thoughts and refocus on the issue at hand. Your calm presence will encourage mutual respect and solution-focused dialogue.

Use "I" statements: You represent You. No one else. Express how the situation affects you and if you are the leader, how it impacted the team, using statements like, "I've noticed this project quality has not matched your previous work, which is impacting the team's progress. Can we talk about what's going on and how it can be fixed?" This approach reduces the chances of the individual feeling blamed or attacked.

Leadership Tip: Frame feedback with "I" statements to express concern without blame. For example, say, "I noticed this task wasn't completed on time, and it's affecting the team's progress. Let's discuss how we can address this together." This approach opens the door for collaboration and problem-solving. This approach does not imply that you will take on the work alone but it does reinforce the team.

Leadership Basics

Focus on solutions: Shift the conversation to finding solutions, even if they are difficult. Work with the person to come up with a plan of action and offer support to help them improve. If you have hired and trained the right team member, they may need some minor mentoring, but solving the problem should be their role and they should own it.

Leadership Tip: Collaboratively set SMART (Specific, Measurable, Achievable, Relevant, Time-bound) goals for improvement. Clear expectations prevent confusion and hold everyone accountable.

Follow up: After the conversation, follow up to ensure the agreed-upon actions are being implemented. This shows commitment to helping the person improve and reinforces accountability.

Leadership Tip: Schedule a check-in within a week or two to review progress on agreed actions. Use this opportunity to provide additional support, acknowledge improvements, and adjust plans if needed. Consistent follow-ups build trust and drive results.

Be Real, Be Direct, Be Authentic, Be Kind.

Getting To "Real"

For many years of my career, I was a "Yes Man." I did whatever my boss wanted, never offering my opinions or ideas. This approach ultimately hindered my growth.

Jon Doolen

Leadership Basics

My leaders never saw what I had to offer because I never showed it. I was solely focused on keeping my bosses happy. They gave me plenty of opportunities to contribute, but I held back. Because they were amazing leaders, I minimized myself to their authority instead of accepting the trust they placed in me, by hiring me.

There was a point in my career when I started reporting to a leadership team without as much experience and training as my previous leaders. It became clear to me very fast that if I did not speak up and offer my opinions and ideas, this team would not survive.

I knew my old approach was dead and I needed to re-invent.

I made a commitment to myself to be open, honest, and transparent with my team and my leaders. I recognized the risk in sharing opposing ideas and philosophies, but more important, I saw the real opportunities LOST because I never spoke up in the past.

I called this new approach "getting to real." It meant moving past the 'nervous new kid' phase, skipping over the 'honeymoon' phase, and putting everything out there, no holding back. The hardest part was overcoming the fear of being judged for sharing an idea that others might scoff at.

Jon Doolen

Leadership Basics

The Power of Open Communication

Fostering a culture of candor has several benefits for both teams and organizations. Here are some key points to consider when adopting this approach:

Promoting Open Communication: Encouraging team members to share ideas openly creates an environment where everyone feels heard and valued. This leads to more innovative solutions and strengthens collaboration.

Leadership Tip: During team meetings, set aside time for a "no idea is a bad idea" brainstorm session to encourage creativity and inclusivity.

Diverse Perspectives: Embracing input from people with different experiences brings fresh perspectives. What might seem like a "crazy" idea can spark breakthrough solutions or inspire more practical alternatives.

Leadership Tip: Seek input from team members who typically stay quiet. Use prompts like, "I'd love to hear your thoughts on this." Inclusive participation generates diverse insights.

Early Idea Screening: Open discussions help identify problematic ideas early on, saving time, resources, and preventing costly mistakes.

Leadership Tip: During brainstorming sessions, ask your team to play the role of a "devil's advocate" for each idea.

Jon Doolen

Leadership Basics

Encourage them to identify potential challenges, risks, or weaknesses early on. This approach fosters critical thinking, refines ideas, and helps avoid costly oversights.

Continuous Improvement: A "getting to real" culture fosters continuous improvement. When everyone is comfortable sharing ideas and challenges, refining strategies over time becomes easier.

Leadership Tip: Schedule regular "reflection sessions" with your team to review what's working and what's not. Ask questions like, "What did we learn this week?" and "What can we improve moving forward?" Encourage openness by modeling vulnerability and sharing your own areas for growth. This creates a safe space for continuous improvement.

Conflict Resolution: Honest communication may lead to conflict, but it also provides a platform for resolving issues constructively. Teams can discuss problems openly and find compromises that work for everyone.

Leadership Tip: When conflicts arise, facilitate a structured discussion where each person involved gets uninterrupted time to share their perspective. Use prompts like, "What do you feel is the main issue?" and "What outcome would you like to see?" Then guide the conversation toward finding common ground and crafting a mutually acceptable solution. This approach ensures all voices are heard and promotes constructive resolution.

Jon Doolen

Leadership Basics

Employee Engagement: When employees feel that their opinions are valued, engagement and job satisfaction rise. People want to contribute meaningfully to the organization's goals.

Leadership Tip: Create a regular feedback loop by implementing "listening sessions" or anonymous surveys where employees can share their ideas and concerns. Follow up by acknowledging the feedback, sharing how it will be acted upon, and crediting employees for their contributions. This demonstrates that their input is valued and fosters deeper engagement.

Things to Keep in Mind

While open communication is key, here are a few considerations:

Balance: It's important to strike a balance between open communication and productivity. Endless discussions without clear action plans can slow down progress.

Leadership Tip: Set a time limit for discussions during meetings and designate a note-taker to document key points. Conclude each discussion with clear action steps, assigning ownership and deadlines to ensure progress while maintaining open communication.

Leadership Basics

Respectful Feedback: Honest feedback should be constructive and respectful. It's about improving ideas, not being blunt or dismissive.

Leadership Tip: When giving feedback, use the "What, Why, How" approach: Clearly state what needs improvement, explain why it's important, and provide suggestions on how to address it. This ensures the feedback is constructive, actionable, and delivered with respect. For example, "Your report missed a few key data points (What). Including them is crucial for accurate decision-making (Why). Let's work together to ensure these are added in future drafts (How)."

Leadership Support: Leaders play a crucial role in creating a culture of openness. They should lead by example and encourage an environment where everyone feels safe to speak their mind.

Leadership Tip: Start team meetings by sharing your own thoughts or challenges openly and honestly. For example, say, "Here's a challenge I'm currently facing, and I'd love your input." This models vulnerability and sets the tone for a culture where others feel safe to express their ideas and concerns. Follow up by actively encouraging participation with prompts like, "What do you think?" or "Does anyone see this differently?"

Continuous Adaptation: Every team is different. What works in one setting might not in another, so be flexible and adapt your approach to fit your team's needs and culture.

Jon Doolen

Leadership Basics

Leadership Tip: Regularly assess your team's dynamics and preferences by conducting short check-ins or pulse surveys. Ask questions like, "What's working well for you?" and "Is there anything we could adjust to improve collaboration?" Use this feedback to tailor your leadership approach, ensuring it aligns with the unique needs and culture of your team. Adapt as needed, and communicate changes openly to maintain trust and engagement.

"Getting to real" in your professional relationships can transform a team's ability to collaborate, solve problems, and innovate. It's a commitment to transparency, constructive communication, and a willingness to be authentic. When done right, it leads to better outcomes, stronger engagement, and a more effective, connected workforce. I found my leadership voice by "getting to real," and it made all the difference.

Conclusion

Effective communication is more than a skill, it is the backbone of impactful leadership. By fostering open dialogue, practicing active listening, and providing constructive feedback, leaders can build trust.

Leaders can resolve conflicts and inspire their teams to achieve shared goals. Clear and empathetic communication ensures that everyone feels heard, valued, and aligned, creating a culture of collaboration and continuous improvement.

Jon Doolen

Leadership Basics

As explored in this chapter, strong communication empowers leaders to navigate challenges, adapt to diverse team dynamics, and motivate others with authenticity and transparency.

By committing to improving their communication strategies, leaders can cultivate stronger connections, drive better results, and leave a lasting positive impact on their teams and organizations.

Leadership Basics

Chapter 7: Building Trust and Credibility

In this chapter, I will discuss the importance of trust and credibility in leadership. Trust and credibility are the cornerstones of effective leadership, forming the foundation for strong relationships with teams, stakeholders, and clients.

Trust enables open communication, collaboration, and loyalty, while credibility enhances a leader's ability to inspire confidence and achieve results. Together, they create the environment necessary for high performance, engagement, and lasting influence.

Through practical leadership tips, this chapter provides the tools to navigate challenges, rebuild trust when it falters, and strengthen the bonds that drive collective success.

The Role of Trust and Credibility in Leadership

Trust and credibility are foundational elements of effective leadership. They serve as the bedrock of relationships between leaders, their teams, stakeholders, and clients. Trust fosters collaboration, loyalty, and high performance, and credibility enhances a leader's influence and ability to achieve results.

Leadership Basics

What is Trust and Why Does It Matter?

Trust is the belief in a leader's reliability, integrity, and competence. It forms the basis of strong, cooperative relationships and is essential for effective teamwork. When team members trust their leader, they are more likely to share ideas, take risks, and work towards common goals.

Trust increases employee engagement and motivation, and it becomes especially crucial during times of change. Leaders who build trust can more easily gain buy-in from their teams, reducing resistance to new initiatives.

Leadership Tip: During times of change, hold regular team updates to clearly explain the reasons behind decisions and provide an opportunity for questions. Transparency reduces uncertainty and builds trust.

What is Credibility and Why Does It Matter?

Credibility is the perception that a leader is knowledgeable, reliable, and trustworthy. It is built over time through consistent actions and ethical behavior.

Credible leaders inspire confidence in their team, attract talent, and are seen as competent in their fields. Credibility drives performance and enhances a leader's reputation both within and outside the organization.

Leadership Tip: To enhance your credibility, regularly share examples of how your decisions are guided by facts,

Jon Doolen

expertise, or team input. Demonstrating thoughtful decision-making builds confidence in your leadership.

How to Build and Maintain Trust and Credibility

Be Transparent: Share information openly and honestly with your team. Transparency builds trust, showing that you have nothing to hide. However, not everything can be shared. When information is private or strategic, be clear about it. For example, say, "I cannot share all the details right now, but I'll provide all the information I can to ensure your success."

Leadership Tip: When transparency is limited, explain why with honesty. Say, "While I can't share every detail, here's what I can tell you and how it impacts our goals." This keeps your team informed and reinforces trust.

Follow Through on Commitments: Consistency between your words and actions reinforces your reliability. Always follow through on promises, no matter how small. When you demonstrate expertise and deliver results, you further strengthen your credibility.

Leadership Tip: Use a task tracker or calendar to ensure you follow through on even small promises. This consistency demonstrates dependability to your team.

Act with Integrity: Always adhere to ethical standards. Integrity builds trust and sets a positive example for your team. Be willing to admit mistakes and take responsibility for your actions.

Leadership Basics

Owning up to errors demonstrates integrity, honesty, accountability, and transparency.

Leadership Tip: When owning up to a mistake, include a clear plan to address it. For example, say, "I missed the deadline, and here's how I'm going to make sure it doesn't happen again." This reinforces accountability and trust.

Be Approachable: Create an open-door policy where team members feel comfortable sharing concerns and ideas. Show empathy by acknowledging their feelings and perspectives. Authentic empathy strengthens relationships and builds trust, helping team members feel valued.

Leadership Tip: Schedule regular one-on-one check-ins with your team to ensure they feel comfortable sharing concerns or ideas. Use these sessions to actively listen and demonstrate empathy.

Encourage Collaboration: Involve your team in decision-making processes. Engaging team members fosters a sense of ownership and trust. As a leader, your success is often magnified when your team wins together. Recognize and appreciate individual contributions, whether they were your ideas or not, to build trust and prevent misunderstandings.

Leadership Tip: During your next team meeting, invite input by asking, "What do you think we could do differently to improve this process?"

Jon Doolen

Leadership Basics

Consistency and Fairness: Treat all team members with fairness and consistency. Clear, consistent communication about expectations, goals, and feedback helps prevent misunderstandings.

While high performers may receive extra benefits or privileges, ensure transparency and clear communication to avoid resentment. There is nothing wrong with high performers getting more, just be honest about it and clearly communicate the path for everyone to earn the extra benefits or privileges.

Leadership Tip: Create a clear performance roadmap that outlines how team members can achieve higher benefits. This transparency prevents misunderstandings and resentment.

Dealing with Trust Issues

Identify the Root Cause: Understand the issue and take time to investigate the underlying causes of the trust problem. Open conversations with those involved can help uncover the real issues.

Leadership Tip: When trust is broken, ask open-ended questions like, "What do you feel has led to this issue?" Listening without defensiveness helps uncover underlying problems.

Address Trust Issues Promptly: Do not delay addressing trust issues. The longer they are left unresolved, the deeper the distrust becomes. Take responsibility for your part in the issue and engage in an honest conversation.

Leadership Tip: Set a time frame for addressing trust issues. For example, schedule a follow-up meeting within a week to discuss progress and show your commitment to resolving the problem.

Acknowledge the Breach: If trust has been broken, acknowledge it and take responsibility. Apologize sincerely. This demonstrates integrity and a commitment to repairing the relationship. Be real about the breach. If the breach caused unfixable damage to the relationship, own it.

Sometimes, time away even if in the form of a breakup, suspension, resignation or termination may be needed. Time apart can sometimes fix the relationship long term. Staying in a low trust environment almost always breeds toxicity.

Leadership Tip: When apologizing, explicitly state what you're apologizing for and how you plan to rebuild trust. For example, say, "I understand that my actions caused confusion, and I'm committed to improving communication moving forward."

Create a Safe Environment: Foster open and honest communication where team members feel safe to express concerns and feedback. Show that you value their input and are willing to make changes based on their suggestions.

Leadership Basics

Leadership Tip: During team meetings, encourage anonymous feedback by using a suggestion box or digital survey. This ensures everyone feels safe to voice concerns.

Rebuild Trust through Consistent Actions: Rebuilding trust requires demonstrating change through consistent actions. Be transparent, deliver on your promises, and engage more with your team to show your commitment to improving.

Leadership Tip: Set measurable goals to demonstrate progress in rebuilding trust. For example, commit to weekly updates or specific deliverables to show reliability over time.

Promote Team Building: Engage in team-building activities to strengthen relationships within the team. As a leader, participate actively, and demonstrate a collaborative culture. This helps team members feel connected and supported, which ultimately strengthens trust.

Leadership Tip: Plan quarterly team-building events focused on collaboration, such as problem-solving challenges. Participate actively to model the collaborative culture you want to build.

Conclusion

Trust and credibility are not just leadership assets, they are necessities for building strong, high-performing teams and fostering meaningful relationships.

Leaders who consistently act with integrity, follow through on commitments, and communicate openly create an environment where collaboration and loyalty thrive.

While trust can take time to build, it can be quickly lost, making it essential for leaders to address issues promptly and demonstrate their reliability through consistent actions.

Credibility further enhances a leader's ability to inspire confidence and drive results. By prioritizing these qualities and applying the strategies outlined in this chapter, leaders can cultivate a culture of trust, accountability, and engagement, paving the way for sustainable success and long-term influence.

Chapter 8: Leading Diverse Teams

In this chapter, I will explore how leading diverse teams offers a powerful advantage in today's dynamic workplace, where varied perspectives, experiences, and skills drive creativity, innovation, and problem-solving.

Diversity enhances decision-making, adaptability, and engagement, enabling organizations to navigate complex challenges with a broader and more informed approach. However, the benefits of diverse teams also come with unique challenges, such as communication barriers, resistance to change, and unconscious biases.

Inclusive leadership plays a pivotal role in fostering an environment where differences are celebrated, and team members feel valued and respected. By understanding and addressing these challenges through open dialogue, cultural awareness, and equitable practices, leaders can unlock the full potential of their teams and create a workplace culture that thrives on collaboration, innovation, and mutual respect.

This chapter explores the benefits, challenges, and strategies for effectively leading diverse teams, with practical tips to apply these principles in real-world scenarios.

Benefits of Leading Diverse Teams

Diverse teams bring a wealth of perspectives, experiences, and skills that can drive innovation and improve decision-making. Here are some of the benefits of leading diverse teams:

Enhanced Creativity and Innovation: Diverse teams are more likely to generate creative ideas, as each member brings unique experiences to the table. These different perspectives contribute to a broader range of ideas, which can lead to innovative solutions to problems. Diverse teams consider a wider array of options, resulting in more informed decision-making and reducing the risk of groupthink.

Leadership Tip: During brainstorming sessions, ensure every team member has a chance to contribute by using a round-robin format or anonymous idea submissions. This encourages participation and leverages diverse perspectives.

Better Decision-Making: Diversity encourages teams to consider a variety of viewpoints, leading to more comprehensive decision-making. The broader range of ideas and approaches reduces the risk of overlooking important factors and helps the team respond more effectively to challenges.

Leadership Tip: Before making a major decision, ask your team to identify potential risks or alternative viewpoints.

Improved Adaptability: Diverse teams are more adaptable to change and better equipped to navigate global markets. Their varied experiences and perspectives help them respond to different challenges and opportunities in ways that a less diverse team might not be able to.

Leadership Tip: Assign team members with different cultural or professional backgrounds to lead global projects or client interactions. Their unique perspectives will improve adaptability and decision-making.

Increased Engagement and Retention: An inclusive leadership style fosters a sense of belonging and respect, which can enhance employee engagement and retention. When team members feel accepted and valued, they are more likely to stay motivated and committed to the organization. In my experience, celebrating and exploring each other's unique backgrounds can help build very strong, cohesive teams.

Leadership Tip: Host regular team-building events where members share their cultural or personal traditions. This fosters mutual respect and a deeper sense of belonging.

Challenges of Leading Diverse Teams

Leading diverse teams also presents unique challenges because we, as individuals, can only experience life through the lens of our own background, no matter how much effort we put into understanding differences.

However, learning about differences and fostering inclusive leadership is essential for leveraging the strengths of diverse team members to maximize success.

It's important to note that these challenges are not necessarily based on race, religion, or gender, but rather the subtle differences in how we communicate and perceive the world around us.

Here are some examples of challenges diverse teams face:

Communication Barriers: The most common challenge is communication. This isn't just about language differences, although that's a factor, but also about differing communication styles. Even two people who grew up in the same town and speak the same language can have diverse ways of expressing themselves based on their backgrounds and life experiences.

Misunderstandings and misinterpretations are inevitable when people come from different cultural contexts.

One of the greatest barriers to communication is fear. Many leaders and staff alike fear having open conversations about diversity at the risk of offending.

Leadership Tip: Begin diversity discussions with ground rules for respect and active listening. For example, ask the team to approach these conversations with curiosity rather than judgment, and ensure everyone has an opportunity to share.

Leadership Basics

Fostering open and respectful discussions about diversity in the workplace is a critical step toward building a stronger, more inclusive environment.

Leaders and team members alike should feel encouraged to engage in conversations about differences in race, religion, gender, age, and other unique aspects that shape our perspectives and experiences.

By approaching these topics with curiosity, education, and respect, we can create a business culture where diversity is not just acknowledged but celebrated. These conversations should focus on understanding, breaking down stereotypes, and finding common ground while honoring the individuality each person brings to the table.

Together, we can build a workplace that thrives on the strength of its differences and the unity of its purpose.

Resistance to Change: Building a diverse team can be difficult because some team members may resist working in a diverse environment due to preconceived biases or a preference for people they perceive as "like them." This resistance can create tension and hinder team cohesion. Effective conflict management techniques are essential to address and resolve these tensions.

Leadership Tip: Address resistance by sharing stories or data about the success of diverse teams. Highlight specific examples where diversity led to better outcomes to inspire buy-in from team members.

Leadership Basics

Unconscious Biases: Unconscious biases are automatic, unintentional judgments or stereotypes we form about people, groups, or situations based on our past experiences, cultural upbringing, or societal influences. These biases occur outside of our conscious awareness and can influence our decisions, actions, and interactions without us realizing it.

Unconscious biases are often linked to factors like race, gender, age, appearance, education, and socioeconomic status, among others. They are shaped by the brain's tendency to categorize information quickly for efficiency, but this can lead to unfair assumptions or behaviors.

Leadership Tip: Conduct a team exercise where members anonymously identify potential biases in decision-making processes. Use the feedback to create standardized, objective criteria for evaluations, hiring, and promotions.

Examples of Unconscious Biases

- **Affinity Bias:** Preferring people who are similar to us in background, interests, or appearance.

- **Confirmation Bias:** Favoring information that supports our existing beliefs while ignoring contrary evidence.

- **Halo Effect:** Assuming someone is good at everything because they excel in one area.

Leadership Basics

- **Gender Bias:** Stereotyping abilities or roles based on someone's gender.
- **Age Bias:** Making assumptions about someone's abilities or value based on their age.

Why It Matters

Unconscious biases can affect decision-making in critical areas like hiring, promotions, teamwork, and customer interactions.

Left unchecked, they can lead to inequity, reduce diversity, and harm workplace culture.

How to Mitigate Unconscious Bias

- **Awareness:** Acknowledge that everyone has biases and commit to recognizing them.
- **Training:** Participate in unconscious bias training to identify and address stereotypes.
- **Standardized Processes:** Use objective criteria for decision-making (e.g., structured interviews for hiring).
- **Diverse Perspectives:** Seek input from a variety of individuals to challenge assumptions.

Leadership Basics

- **Self-Reflection:** Regularly examine your own judgments and ask, *"Why am I making this decision?"*

Understanding and addressing unconscious biases helps foster fairness, inclusivity, and better decision-making in all areas of life.

Unconscious biases, whether based on race, gender, or other factors, can affect decision-making and interactions within the team.

Even teams that look similar on the surface still have biases that can influence behavior and outcomes. Leaders need to be aware of these biases and work to mitigate their impact. Addressing unconscious bias is critical to fostering an inclusive team culture.

Strategies for Understanding Individual Differences

Awareness Training: While many corporate diversity programs focus on race, religion, or gender, the best programs dive deeper into individual differences. If you have influence over these programs, ensure they offer comprehensive training that educates team members about diverse communication styles, customs, and cultural practices.

Leadership Tip: Partner with a diversity expert to deliver hands-on training sessions, including role-playing

Leadership Basics

exercises to help the team practice navigating individual differences in real scenarios.

Get to Know Your Team: Never assume that just because someone looks like you, they think like you. Don't assume that what you find funny, they will find funny. Take the time to learn about your team members' backgrounds and experiences. Ask questions, listen to answers, and celebrate the uniqueness of each person on your team.

Leadership Tip: Dedicate time during meetings to a "sharing moment" where a team member shares a tradition, holiday, or personal experience. This builds understanding and camaraderie.

Encourage Open Dialogue: Create an environment where team members feel comfortable sharing their backgrounds. This open dialogue promotes understanding, reduces misunderstandings, and builds stronger relationships within the team.

Leadership Tip: Use anonymous feedback tools to allow team members to voice concerns or suggestions about diversity efforts without fear of judgment. Follow up on the feedback to demonstrate your commitment to inclusivity.

Adapt Your Leadership Style: Adapt your approach to accommodate your team members, they are not the same, they are each unique. This might involve adjusting communication styles, decision-making processes, or how you celebrate achievements within the team.

Leadership Tip: Use tools like DISC or Myers-Briggs assessments to identify communication preferences within your team and tailor your approach to suit their needs.

Celebrate Cultural Diversity: Recognize and celebrate cultural diversity by encouraging team members to share their traditions and cultural holidays. Promoting cultural exchange strengthens the team's sense of belonging and appreciation for one another.

Leadership Tip: Host a quarterly cultural appreciation day where team members can showcase food, music, or traditions from their backgrounds. This fosters inclusivity and learning.

Promote Equity and Fairness: Ensure that all team members have equal opportunities for growth and development. Address any disparities in treatment and ensure that rewards and recognition are based on performance, not favoritism. Refer back to the section of the chapter regarding unconscious bias.

Leadership Tip: Regularly review team performance data to identify disparities in promotions or rewards. Address any gaps by implementing clear, objective criteria for advancement.

Leadership Basics

How to Leverage the Strengths of Diverse Team Members

Identify Individual Strengths: Take the time to understand each team member's unique skills and strengths. Use tools such as personality assessments, skill inventories, and performance reviews to identify these strengths and maximize their potential.

Leadership Tip: Use personality and skill tests like StrengthsFinder to create a team strengths map. Share the map with the team to encourage collaboration based on complementary skills.

Assign Roles Strategically: Align team roles with individual strengths to enhance overall team performance. This ensures that each team member is contributing in the best way possible and maximizes the collective strength of the group.

Leadership Tip: Rotate roles occasionally to give team members opportunities to explore new areas and uncover hidden talents while keeping projects fresh.

Encourage Collaboration: Foster collaboration by encouraging knowledge-sharing and cross-functional projects. Diverse teams thrive when they can leverage each other's strengths, share ideas, and collaborate to solve problems.

Jon Doolen

Leadership Basics

Leadership Tip: Pair team members from different departments or backgrounds to work on projects together. Cross-functional collaboration enhances learning and problem-solving.

Provide Opportunities for Growth: Encourage continuous improvement and personal development. Offer mentorship programs, leadership development opportunities, and other resources that help team members develop their skills and advance their careers.

Leadership Tip: Create a mentorship program where senior team members from diverse backgrounds mentor junior colleagues. This fosters growth and builds a pipeline of future leaders.

Acknowledge Achievements: Recognize and celebrate the contributions of diverse team members. Publicly acknowledging their efforts not only boosts morale but also reinforces a culture of inclusivity and appreciation.

Leadership Tip: Use team meetings to spotlight individual contributions and explain how they benefited the group. Public recognition builds morale and reinforces inclusivity.

Conclusion

Leading diverse teams is both a responsibility and an opportunity for modern leaders. Diversity fosters creativity, innovation, and better decision-making by bringing together

Leadership Basics

unique perspectives and experiences. However, realizing these benefits requires intentional effort to address communication barriers, unconscious biases, and resistance to change.

Inclusive leadership, rooted in empathy, equity, and open dialogue, creates an environment where team members feel valued and empowered to contribute their best.

By celebrating differences, promoting cultural understanding, and leveraging individual strengths, leaders can build cohesive teams that thrive on collaboration and mutual respect. Ultimately, the success of a diverse team depends on a leader's commitment to fostering inclusivity and embracing the potential that diversity offers to create stronger, more dynamic organizations.

Jon Doolen

Chapter 9: Conflict Resolution and Negotiation

In this chapter, we will explore the benefits and techniques of managing conflicts within teams. Conflict is an inevitable part of teamwork, but identifying and addressing it effectively can make the difference between a thriving or dysfunctional team.

Signs of conflict can range from reduced performance and morale to more visible issues like interpersonal tension or even unexpected resignations. Left unaddressed, these tensions can escalate, damaging productivity and relationships within the team.

Leaders play a critical role in spotting early warning signs, such as changes in collaboration patterns or the formation of cliques. Leaders are also responsible for creating an environment where open dialogue can prevent issues from festering.

By addressing conflicts promptly, fostering a culture of psychological safety, and employing structured conflict resolution techniques, leaders can transform challenges into opportunities for growth and cohesion.

Through careful observation, one-on-one check-ins, and tools like mediation and negotiation strategies, leaders can not only resolve conflicts but also strengthen trust and collaboration within their teams.

Jon Doolen

Leadership Basics

This chapter explores practical strategies for identifying, managing, and resolving team conflicts to create a healthier and more productive workplace.

Identifying Conflicts Within Teams

Conflicts often manifest in observable signs, such as increased stress, changes in communication patterns, or visible discomfort among team members. However, sometimes conflicts are harder to detect until they impact performance directly. Common early signs of conflict include:

- **Reduced performance**: Declines in sales, missed goals, or a decrease in productivity.
- **Unexpected resignations**: A team member leaving unexpectedly can be a sign of unresolved tension.
- **Physical altercations**: The most extreme sign of conflict, often a result of prolonged unresolved tensions.

In many cases, these signs arise because conflicts have been ignored or avoided. When conflicts are not addressed promptly, they escalate. Ignoring the issue, or assuming it will resolve itself, is a weak leadership tactic.

Leadership Tip: Schedule monthly team check-ins focused on team dynamics. Use anonymous surveys or one-on-one discussions to identify potential tension points before they escalate.

Leadership Basics

Leadership involves actively observing team dynamics and addressing tensions early.

How to Spot Conflict Early

- **Behavioral changes**: Watch for team members avoiding each other or reacting negatively to specific topics.

Leadership Tip: Keep a leadership journal to document observed behavioral patterns and subtle changes in team dynamics. Review these notes weekly to identify trends.

- **Lack of collaboration**: Reduced teamwork or reluctance to cooperate often signals underlying issues.

Leadership Tip: Schedule a team meeting or one-on-one conversations to identify barriers to collaboration. Ask open-ended questions like, "What's been challenging about working together lately?" Actively listen, address concerns, and clarify expectations to rebuild trust and teamwork.

- **Subgroup formation**: Pay attention to cliques or subgroups forming within the team, which can indicate hidden conflicts.

Leadership Tip: When noticing cliques, assign cross-functional projects that require team members to

Leadership Basics

collaborate outside their usual groups to rebuild cohesion.

It's also important to monitor performance and morale. Sudden changes in key performance indicators (KPIs), employee satisfaction, or engagement levels may point to unresolved conflicts.

A simple, non-confrontational conversation can help gauge the situation before it becomes a bigger issue.

Techniques for Resolving Conflicts

Addressing Issues Early: The sooner you address a conflict, the easier it is to prevent escalation. Early intervention can show your team that you are paying attention and committed to finding a resolution.

However, not everyone processes conflict the same way, so be mindful of the pace at which you address issues. If you rush to resolve it, it may escalate the situation further. Allow some team members time to cool off before re-engaging.

Leadership Tip: Use a conflict resolution checklist during early intervention to ensure key points are addressed, such as acknowledging the issue, listening to all parties, and defining next steps.

One-on-One Check-ins: Conduct regular check-ins with team members, blending business and personal conversations. This allows for deeper connections and helps build trust.

These conversations also create a foundation for when conflict arises. When leaders only approach team members during issues, they reinforce a relationship based on negativity, not trust.

Leadership Tip: Use a structured yet flexible template for check-ins that includes questions about workload, team dynamics, and personal development. For example: "What's going well? What could improve? How can I support you?"

Creating a Safe Environment: Your office or meeting space should feel like a safe environment where team members can express concerns without fear of judgment or reprisal. If every meeting is seen as disciplinary, team members may avoid discussing problems with you.

Encourage open dialogue by making these spaces comfortable for casual and important conversations alike.

Practice active listening during these discussions to show empathy and understanding.

Leadership Tip: At the start of meetings, establish psychological safety by saying, "This is a space for open and respectful conversations. All feedback is valuable, and no ideas are off-limits."

Leadership Basics

Mediation and Third-Party Facilitation: Sometimes, conflicts are too intense for direct resolution, and a neutral third party can help. If you are involved in the conflict, consider using an outside mediator to facilitate discussions. If a conflict involves several team members, a trained mediator can ensure productive discussions and help find common ground.

Leadership Tip: Partner with HR or external consultants to develop a pre-approved list of mediators who can be brought in quickly when conflicts escalate beyond internal resolution.

Negotiation Skills for Leaders

When you find yourself in the middle of a negotiation, here are some strategies to stay on track:

Prepare Thoroughly: Understand the issues, gather information, and talk to everyone involved to see all perspectives.

Leadership Tip: Before addressing a conflict, create a "perspective map" where you list the concerns or viewpoints of everyone involved. Use this to identify common ground or recurring themes that can guide the resolution process.

Set Clear Objectives: Define clear objectives and desired outcomes before entering negotiations. If you're not fully

Leadership Basics

involved in the process, build rapport with all parties to avoid perceptions of favoritism.

Leadership Tip: Use SMART goals (Specific, Measurable, Achievable, Relevant, Time-bound) to define your objectives and communicate them clearly during the negotiation process.

Build Rapport: Establish trust by being honest, open, and respectful. Acknowledging areas of agreement can help ease the tension and create a more cooperative atmosphere.

Leadership Tip: Start conflict resolution meetings by highlighting areas of agreement, such as shared goals or mutual interests. For example, say, "We all agree that meeting this deadline is important, let's work together to figure out how we can achieve it." This builds rapport and sets a collaborative tone.

Communicate Effectively: Use "I" statements to express your perspective without sounding accusatory. Active listening is crucial to show engagement and understanding.

Leadership Tip: Practice active listening by summarizing what you hear during negotiations. For instance, say, "Here's what I'm hearing. Is that correct?" This approach shows engagement and builds trust.

Leadership Basics

Explore Interests, Not Positions: Focus on the underlying interests of the parties involved rather than their fixed positions. This helps identify mutually beneficial solutions.

Leadership Tip: During conflict discussions, ask open-ended questions like, "What's most important to you in this situation?" This shifts the focus from rigid positions to underlying interests, paving the way for solutions that work for everyone.

Aim for Win-Win Solutions: Look for solutions that meet the interests of all parties, even if the solution is not immediately apparent. Sometimes the right answer involves compromise and creative solutions.

Leadership Tip: When resolving conflicts, ask both parties, "What does a successful outcome look like for you?" Use their responses to brainstorm creative compromises that address key interests on both sides, ensuring a win-win solution.

Adapt Strategies: Be flexible in your approach as new information comes in. Stay calm and professional, and be prepared to defend your ideas by exploring their potential weaknesses.

Leadership Tip: During discussions, regularly pause to ask, "Has anything new come to light that changes how we should approach this?" Staying open to updates ensures your strategy remains flexible and relevant.

Leadership Basics

Manage Emotions: Maintain a professional demeanor, keeping emotions in check for both yourself and the team. Managing emotions is key to preventing escalation and maintaining a calm atmosphere.

Leadership Tip: When emotions run high, take a moment to pause, breathe deeply, and refocus before responding. Encourage your team to do the same by saying, "Let's take a brief moment to collect our thoughts and approach this calmly."

Make Concessions Wisely: Make concessions on less critical issues to gain ground on more important matters. Ensure that concessions are reciprocated to maintain a fair negotiation process.

Leadership Tip: Identify less critical points before entering a negotiation and be ready to offer concessions on those. For example, say, "I'm willing to adjust the timeline slightly if we can agree on maintaining the budget," ensuring fairness and reciprocity in the process.

Close the Deal: Clearly summarize the agreed-upon terms and follow up to ensure compliance. Address any emerging issues quickly to maintain a positive outcome.

Leadership Tip: At the end of a meeting or negotiation, summarize the agreed terms in writing and share them with all parties involved. For example, send a follow-up email outlining responsibilities, deadlines, and next steps to ensure alignment and accountability. Address any questions or issues promptly to keep progress on track.

Building Conflict Resolution Guidelines

Establish clear conflict resolution policies within your team. Everyone should be aware of acceptable behaviors and procedures for resolving conflicts. Regularly review these guidelines with your team and ensure they are enforced consistently.

Create a Code of Conduct: This should outline the behaviors expected of team members and the processes for resolving conflicts.

Leadership Tip: Share the code of conduct at onboarding and review it quarterly during team meetings to reinforce expectations and address questions.

Enforce Fairness: Apply conflict resolution policies consistently, addressing any disparities in treatment or behavior. Keep in mind that high performance perks do not always translate into unfairness.

Leadership Tip: During conflict resolution, ensure that all team members understand and adhere to the same policies. For example, if a high performer is given additional flexibility, transparently communicate the reasons behind it and outline how others can achieve similar benefits. Consistent application of policies builds trust and fairness within the team.

Support a Healthy Work Environment: Monitor the progress of conflict resolution and offer support to team members as needed to prevent future issues.

Leadership Tip: Use anonymous post-conflict resolution surveys to gather feedback on the effectiveness of the process and make improvements where necessary.

Conclusion

Effectively managing team conflicts is a vital leadership skill that requires attentiveness, empathy, and strategic action. Conflict, when handled constructively, can serve as a catalyst for growth, innovation, and stronger team dynamics. By identifying early warning signs, fostering open communication, and employing structured resolution strategies, leaders can prevent minor disagreements from escalating into major issues.

Building a culture of trust, fairness, and psychological safety ensures that team members feel valued and empowered to address challenges collaboratively. By embracing conflict as an opportunity rather than a setback, leaders can create an environment where diverse perspectives thrive and teams achieve their full potential.

Successful conflict resolution is not just about restoring harmony, it's about fostering stronger relationships and paving the way for long-term success.

Leadership Basics

Chapter 10: Building and Sustaining Relationships

In this chapter, we will explore the importance of relationships in leadership. Effective leadership isn't just about managing tasks, it's about building trust and credibility with your team.

When leaders foster strong, authentic relationships, they create an environment where team members feel safe to share ideas, take risks, and collaborate, ultimately driving success. Trust is the foundation of these relationships, and without it, team performance suffers.

This chapter delves into the critical role of relationships in leadership, particularly through tools like one-on-one meetings, which provide a space for open communication, coaching, and alignment.

Strong relationships not only enhance teamwork and innovation but also increase employee retention and engagement. Whether through scheduled meetings or casual interactions, cultivating meaningful connections empowers teams to perform at their best.

Jon Doolen

Leadership Basics

Why Should You Care About Relationships in Leadership?

Strong relationships are built on trust and credibility. Trust is the foundation of any meaningful relationship. When leaders build trust with their team members, they create an environment where people feel safe to express ideas, take risks, and collaborate effectively.

Leaders who are trusted gain the respect and loyalty of their team members and stakeholders, which is essential for achieving success.

Your team is unlikely to work at their full potential for you if they don't trust you. They need to know who you are, how you process information, and how you react to events. To achieve this, you must let them in. Start conversations, listen to them, and let them be vulnerable.

Occasionally, you should also share something personal to deepen the connection. Building these relationships will create a stronger team and boost overall performance.

Leadership Tip: Building trust begins with being authentic. Start small, show your human side and let others in, even if it's just sharing something personal. It's these small actions that help lay the foundation for trust.

Jon Doolen

Leadership Basics

The One-on-One

There are several ways for you to earn their trust. One of the most reliable ways and one of the most avoided tools in a leaders tool box, is the one-on-one meeting.

A one-on-one is a dedicated, usually scheduled meeting between a leader (such as a manager, supervisor, or coach) and an individual team member.

It's a private, uninterrupted time for open communication, relationship-building, and addressing both professional and personal development.

Key Features of a One-on-One:

Personalized Attention: The meeting focuses solely on the team member, their needs, goals, and concerns.

Regularly Scheduled: Typically held weekly, bi-weekly, or monthly to create consistency and build trust.

Two-Way Dialogue: It's not just the leader talking. Both parties share insights, give feedback, and exchange ideas.
Customized Agenda: While topics may vary, they often include updates on work progress, career development, challenges, and feedback.

Private and Confidential: It's a safe space where sensitive or personal topics can be discussed freely.

Leadership Basics

Leadership Tip: Make it personal. A one-on-one isn't just about discussing work, it's a chance to connect as humans. Use this time to get to know your team members, their challenges, and their goals.

Purpose of a One-on-One:

- Strengthen the relationship between the leader and the team member.
- Provide clarity on goals, expectations, and priorities.
- Offer coaching, mentorship, and guidance.
- Address concerns or challenges early.
- Celebrate achievements and recognize contributions.
- Discuss personal career development and growth opportunities.

Leadership Tip: Always be present and actively listen. This not only helps your team member feel valued, but it also provides invaluable insights into their motivations and obstacles.

Example Topics in a One-on-One:

- Current work progress and roadblocks.
- Feedback on performance (both giving and receiving).
- Career aspirations and skill development.
- Personal challenges impacting work.
- Ideas or suggestions for team improvement.

Leadership Basics

One-on-ones are a simple but powerful tool for fostering trust, alignment, and growth between leaders and their teams. It's about more than tasks; it's about people. One-on-one meetings are the backbone of strong relationships between leaders and their team members. Here's why they're so critical:

Personal Connection: One-on-ones create a space for personalized communication, showing team members that their leader values them as individuals, not just workers. This connection fosters trust and loyalty.

Clarity and Alignment: These meetings ensure alignment on goals, expectations, and priorities. Subordinates can share updates, ask questions, and get clear on how their work ties to the bigger picture.

Open Communication: They provide a safe, private environment for team members to discuss concerns, share feedback, or propose ideas without fear of judgment or interruption.

Coaching and Development: Leaders can use one-on-ones to mentor, coach, and support their team's professional growth, tailoring guidance to each person's needs and goals.

Recognition and Motivation: Recognizing effort and celebrating wins—big or small—during one-on-ones boosts morale and reinforces desired behaviors.

Leadership Basics

Problem Solving: These sessions allow for early identification and resolution of challenges, preventing small issues from growing into bigger problems.

Empowerment: When leaders actively listen and encourage team members to share their insights, it empowers them to take ownership of their roles and decisions.

Feedback Flow: It's a two-way street. Leaders can give constructive feedback while receiving valuable input about their leadership style and decisions.

Ultimately, one-on-ones build the foundation of trust, understanding, and collaboration. It's not just about the work, it's about the relationship, and those connections are what drive engagement, retention, and performance.

One-on-one meetings don't always have to be formal or scheduled to make a difference, they can happen in the small, seemingly casual moments throughout the day. A quick fly-by conversation, a check-in while grabbing coffee, or even a brief pause during a busy shift can create opportunities for team members to share their thoughts, ask questions, or raise concerns. These informal touchpoints show that you're approachable and invested in their success, creating a sense of connection and trust.

By taking even a few minutes to give your undivided attention, you open the door for honest communication, build rapport, and address issues before they escalate. It's not about the structure, it's about the intentional effort to show you're there for your team.

The Impact of Strong Relationships

Encouraging Cooperation and Teamwork: Leaders who foster strong relationships can bring people together to work toward common goals. This applies not only within your team but also with other departments, vendors, clients, and external partners.

Facilitating Open Communication: When there are strong relationships, communication becomes more transparent and honest. This reduces misunderstandings and fosters a culture of openness. Employees who have good relationships with their leaders are more engaged and motivated to contribute to the organization's success.

Enhancing Employee Retention: Strong relationships contribute to higher retention rates. When employees feel connected to their leaders, they are more likely to stay with the organization. People leave jobs for many reasons, but don't let it be because you failed to build a relationship with them. Many people believe and some studies have supported that one of the top reasons someone leaves an employer is their direct leadership. Building strong relationships cannot be stressed enough here.

Driving Innovation and Growth: Leaders who have built relationships based on trust and respect create environments where creativity can thrive. When team members feel valued, they are more likely to share their ideas, leading to innovation and organizational growth. Strong relationships also provide access to a broader network of resources, knowledge, and opportunities, which benefits both personal and organizational development.

Leadership Tip: Focus on building relationships that foster mutual respect, not just compliance. When people trust and respect you, they're more likely to go the extra mile to help you succeed.

Networking Strategies for Leaders

Networking is a key part of leadership and building relationships. Here are some strategies I recommend:

Be Genuine and Authentic: Build relationships based on real interest and authenticity. People can tell when interactions are insincere, and this can damage trust. Get to know others' interests, values, and goals. This fosters deeper connections and mutual respect.

Acknowledge Your Weaknesses: If you struggle with remembering names or personal details, be upfront about it. Let people know you might need reminders and show genuine interest in their lives. This honesty builds authenticity and strengthens relationships.

Cultivate a Diverse Network: Engage with people from different industries, backgrounds, and levels of experience. A diverse network provides varied perspectives and valuable resources. Attend industry events, participate in networking groups, and

Leadership Basics

make connections both online and offline.

Leverage LinkedIn: Use LinkedIn to connect with professionals in your field. Share relevant content, engage in discussions, and join industry-specific groups to grow your online presence.

After connecting, take the initiative to get on a quick call with new contacts to offer your support and start a dialogue. Follow people, be ok with followers. Don't be scared to connect and communicate. LinkedIn is no longer only a job search web site.

Share articles or posts that align with your leadership style. As often as possible, keep content neutral to encourage participation and engagement. Engaging with others' content on social media is also key, comment positively and thoughtfully, even when you disagree.

Support Others in Your Network: Building a reputation as a reliable and helpful contact strengthens relationships. Share your knowledge, offer advice, and support others without expecting immediate returns.

Know When to Set Limits: Be mindful of how much time and expertise you give away for free. Offer value, but be conscious of your boundaries, especially when it comes to providing professional services outside your organization's business model.

Follow Up and Maintain Contact: After meeting new contacts, follow up with a personalized message to solidify the connection. Keep in touch periodically, ask how they're doing, and offer help where needed.

Leadership Tip: Networking isn't just about gathering business cards. Focus on genuine, long-term relationships. Be proactive in helping others without expecting immediate returns.

Turning New Contacts into Long-Term Relationships

Consistency and Reliability: Be dependable and follow through on commitments. Regular interactions help keep relationships strong. Regularly express gratitude and appreciation for the support your network provides. Simple gestures like thank-you notes go a long way in building trust.

Celebrate Milestones: Acknowledge achievements and successes in your network. Recognizing milestones not only strengthens your relationship but also fosters goodwill. A simple text or message to congratulate someone on a professional achievement can make a lasting impact.

Adapt and Evolve: Stay informed about industry changes and the professional lives of your contacts. Be flexible in how you connect with others, embracing new tools and communication methods to stay engaged.

Personalize Interactions: Remembering personal details like birthdays or special events adds a personal touch to your professional relationships. Use technology to track these moments and make your contacts feel valued.

Prioritize Face-to-Face Meetings: When possible, meet in person. Face-to-face conversations create deeper connections and help build stronger relationships. Even virtual meetings can deepen bonds, but there's nothing quite like an in-person conversation.

Address Conflicts Gracefully: If conflicts arise, address them promptly. Open communication and finding common ground are essential for maintaining long-term relationships. Sometimes, just listening and acknowledging another person's perspective can de-escalate a situation.

Respect Boundaries: Be mindful of others' boundaries. Not everyone will be comfortable with constant contact or personal inquiries, and respecting their space shows consideration and respect.

Leadership Tip: Consistency is key. Don't let relationships fizzle out after a single conversation. Follow up, stay engaged, and always add value to those connections.

Conclusion

In leadership, the foundation of success lies in the relationships you build with your team. Trust, authenticity, and consistent

Leadership Basics

communication are key to creating an environment where people feel valued and motivated.

One-on-one meetings, both formal and informal, offer invaluable opportunities to connect on a personal level, provide mentorship, and align on goals. These interactions foster openness, build loyalty, and drive performance.

By investing in your relationships - whether through a dedicated meeting or a simple check-in - you empower your team to thrive. Strong relationships not only improve teamwork and communication but also spark innovation and increase retention, all of which contribute to long-term organizational success.

Ultimately, leadership is about more than directing work; it's about creating connections that inspire, support, and drive individuals to achieve their full potential. As you continue to nurture these relationships, you'll find that the trust and respect you've cultivated will be your greatest assets in leading a high-performing team.

Leadership Basics

Chapter 11: Leading Through Change and Crisis

In this chapter, we will discuss how to lead teams through periods of change and crisis. In my leadership journey, I have found that the most defining moments often arise in times of change and crisis. Whether turning around underperforming departments or launching new markets from scratch, I've been called upon to lead when the stakes were highest.

These experiences taught me that effective leadership isn't just about managing the logistics of a crisis; it's about staying present, maintaining morale, and guiding your team with unwavering optimism.

In this chapter, I'll share key lessons I've learned from navigating challenges, such as taking over a struggling division in 2005 and leading through the uncertainty of the COVID-19 pandemic. I'll discuss the strategies that helped us not only survive but thrive during difficult times, focusing on leadership qualities like communication, empathy, and maintaining a sense of purpose.

Whether you're leading through a crisis or managing change, these lessons will provide practical insights on how to support your team, maintain high morale, and steer the ship toward success even in the toughest of times.

Jon Doolen

Leadership Basics

Leading Through Change and Crisis: My Experience

Throughout my career, I've gained much of my leadership experience by stepping into situations requiring change and crisis management. I've often been the "fix-it" person, whether turning around broken departments or launching new markets from scratch, often without immediate support.

In these situations, you learn quickly that maintaining not only your own morale but also keeping your team's spirit high is a defining aspect of leadership.
In 2005, I stepped into a leadership role that many considered a "dead man walking" assignment, following two predecessors who had faced health challenges preventing their return.

The division, with its high stress and complex demands, managed over 1,200 daily customer contacts across three states, a footprint that would expand to 48 states and include international clients under my tenure. Despite the challenges, I saw opportunity and led the team with a foundation of open communication, trust, transparency, and a commitment to continuing education.

Together, we transformed the culture and operations, turning what was once a high-pressure environment into a thriving, collaborative team. The results spoke for themselves as we not only met but exceeded expectations, achieving growth and success that once seemed out of reach.

Jon Doolen

Leadership Basics

During difficult periods, such as the COVID-19 pandemic in 2020, I worked every day, seven days a week, alongside my team, to navigate the numerous challenges. While the furniture industry saw a sales boom due to people staying at home, the uncertainty, fear, and emotional toll on the team were substantial. Acknowledging those emotions while keeping the team on track was crucial.

My team and I listened to their fears, validated their concerns, and focused on keeping the team safe while continuing operations. These experiences taught me that even in the hardest times, you must stay present, support your team emotionally, and lead by example.

Strategies for Leading Through Crisis

Maintain Positivity and Optimism

As a leader of people, you are always on stage, especially during crises. Your team will look to you for direction, and it's critical that you stay positive. Optimism can be contagious and can help lift team spirits. Even if the situation is grim, guiding the team with a hopeful attitude can provide energy to persevere. Celebrate small wins, keep morale high, and focus on the opportunities that can arise from the crisis.

Remind your team of the organization's mission and the bigger picture. When team members see how their individual roles contribute to the overall goal, it can reignite their sense of purpose.

Leadership Basics

Hold Daily "Stand-Up" Meetings

Reinforce purpose and positivity through practical application. In times of crisis, hold short, daily stand-up meetings with your team. Focus on celebrating even small victories, reminding everyone of how their actions contribute to the bigger mission. These meetings should be brief but intentional, highlighting progress, staying positive, and refocusing on the organization's long-term goals.

Why it Works:

- Keeps morale high and helps team members stay engaged and aligned with the bigger picture.
- Reinforces the sense of purpose and shared responsibility.
- Provides a consistent space to celebrate wins and shift focus to opportunities, no matter how small.

Leadership Tip: Make sure the tone is uplifting and hopeful, even when discussing challenges, to model optimism and keep the team motivated.

Over-Communicate and Be Transparent

Communication is essential during times of change. It's important to keep your team informed with regular updates. Even if you don't have all the answers, it's better to communicate uncertainty than to remain silent. Saying nothing often breeds anxiety and speculation.

Jon Doolen

Leadership Basics

Be clear about what you can and cannot share. Transparency builds trust, even if the news isn't positive. Let your team know when they can expect updates and always communicate slightly ahead of that time to ensure you're proactive. Use various communication channels, (like emails, meetings, video calls) to ensure everyone is reached.

Provide Clarity and Direction

In periods of crisis, confusion can easily set in. Ensuring clarity of roles, responsibilities, and next steps is critical. Offer actionable plans and ensure that everyone knows their purpose and goals. This alignment helps prevent misunderstandings and keeps the team focused on solutions.

If your organization has established processes for crisis management, familiarize yourself with them and follow them. If not, create a clear structure to help everyone navigate the challenges ahead.

Creating a crisis management structure from scratch, especially if your organization lacks established processes, is crucial for ensuring everyone knows how to respond when challenges arise.

Here are some steps you can take to create a clear structure:

Leadership Basics

Define What Constitutes a Crisis

- **Identify potential crises**: Start by outlining the types of crises your organization might face (e.g., financial, operational, reputational, natural disasters, cyber threats, etc.).

- **Create crisis categories**: Not all crises are the same, so categorize them based on their severity and impact. This helps prioritize responses.

Leadership Tip: Be Proactive, Not Reactive. Leaders who take a proactive approach reduce the shock and uncertainty when crises arise, allowing for a more controlled and thoughtful response. This helps in setting a tone for the rest of the team.

Establish a Crisis Management Team

- **Select key individuals**: Identify people across departments (e.g., leadership, HR, IT, communications, legal, and operations) who will play critical roles in the crisis response.

- **Designate a crisis leader**: Appoint one person as the head of the crisis management team to ensure coordination and decision-making.

Leadership Tip: Empower and Trust Your Team. Empowering your team not only reduces bottlenecks in decision-making but also boosts morale and

Leadership Basics

performance. This is especially critical in high-pressure crisis situations.

- **Define roles and responsibilities**: Assign specific roles (e.g., communication lead, resource manager, operational coordinator) to ensure no one is left wondering what to do.

Leadership Tip: Delegate with Confidence. Delegating allows leaders to focus on the bigger picture while allowing those with specialized knowledge to handle tasks. It also helps build leadership within the organization.

Develop a Communication Plan

- **Internal communication**: Ensure clear lines of communication with all employees. Determine how information will be shared (e.g., via email, messaging platforms, intranet).

Leadership Tip: Lead with Empathy in Communication. Crisis situations often lead to anxiety or fear. Empathy in communication builds trust and reassures employees and stakeholders that their concerns are understood and valued.

- **External communication**: Decide how to communicate with customers, vendors, and other stakeholders. Designate a spokesperson and develop templates for key messages.

Leadership Basics

- **Regular updates**: Make sure there is a system in place to update all relevant parties regularly during a crisis. This includes tracking progress and addressing concerns.

Leadership Tip: Communicate Transparently and Often. In times of crisis, people crave information. Leaders who communicate openly prevent rumors and confusion, and provide a sense of direction and stability.

Create Crisis Response Procedures

- **Document the steps**: Develop a clear, step-by-step guide on what needs to happen in the event of a crisis. This should cover:
    - Initial assessment and declaration of a crisis
    - Immediate response actions
    - Short- and long-term mitigation strategies

Leadership Tip: Decide Quickly, but Don't Rush. Decisiveness in a crisis is crucial, but rushed decisions can lead to mistakes. Leaders should take the necessary time to gather facts, consult with the team, and then make informed choices.

- **Escalation protocols**: Define how information and issues are escalated. For example, what happens if the crisis reaches a certain threshold (e.g., from department-level management to executive leadership)?

Leadership Basics

Leadership Tip: Maintain Calm Under Pressure. Calm leadership in the face of a crisis sets the tone for the team. It inspires confidence and gives others the clarity they need to perform their roles.

- **Recovery plans**: Detail how the organization will recover after the crisis, including assessing damage, rebuilding systems, and restoring operations.

Train Your Team

- **Crisis drills**: Run regular drills or tabletop exercises to simulate different types of crises. This prepares your team to act quickly and confidently when a real crisis occurs.

Leadership Tip: Lead by Example in Crisis Drills. When leaders engage in crisis simulations, they demonstrate commitment to preparation and resilience, encouraging the same level of involvement from their teams.

- **Cross-training**: Ensure that team members are trained in multiple areas of crisis management so that the burden doesn't fall on one person if a member is unavailable.

Leadership Tip: Promote Continuous Learning. Training should never be one-and-done. By promoting continuous learning, leaders ensure that their teams remain flexible and better prepared for future challenges.

Leadership Basics

- **Empower decision-making**: Train your team to make informed decisions based on predefined guidelines and empower them to act swiftly within their scope of responsibility.

Create a Resource & Support Network

- **Tools and technology**: Make sure you have the right tools in place for managing a crisis, such as project management software, communication tools, and access to emergency resources.

- **External support**: Build relationships with third-party vendors or consultants who can provide external support during a crisis, such as PR firms, legal experts, or IT specialists.

Leadership Tip: Foster a Collaborative Leadership Network. In times of crisis, collaboration with trusted external partners can provide additional resources and support. A leader who networks strategically ensures their team isn't isolated.

Establish a Crisis Evaluation Process

- **Post-crisis review**: After the crisis has passed, conduct a debriefing with your team to evaluate the response. What worked? What didn't? What could have been improved?

Leadership Basics

- **Lessons learned**: Document insights from the evaluation and update the crisis management plan accordingly. This is key to continually improving and ensuring readiness for future crises.

Leadership Tip: Encourage Open Feedback and Accountability. Feedback loops improve future responses, and leaders who create a culture of accountability and openness allow their teams to grow and improve from each crisis.

Build a Culture of Preparedness

- **Encourage proactive problem-solving**: Foster a culture where employees feel comfortable identifying potential issues and raising concerns before they escalate into full-blown crises.

- **Leadership involvement**: Leadership should set the example by being transparent, calm, and solution-oriented in any crisis situation, promoting a sense of unity and resilience.

Leadership Tip: Be Visible and Approachable During Crisis. Visible leadership creates a sense of unity and ensures that leaders are seen as accessible, reinforcing trust and fostering a team-oriented atmosphere.

- **Regular reviews**: Continuously review and refine crisis management plans to adapt to new risks or changing business environments.

Leadership Basics

Leadership Tip: Champion a "Fail Fast, Learn Faster" Mentality. Leaders who promote a mindset where mistakes are viewed as lessons help their teams develop resilience and innovation, making them better prepared for future challenges.

Define Success Metrics

- **Clear criteria for success**: Establish measurable goals for handling crises (e.g., response time, stakeholder satisfaction, recovery time). This will help gauge the effectiveness of your crisis management efforts.

Leadership Tip: Measure Progress, Not Perfection. In a crisis, it's rare to achieve perfect outcomes. Leaders should focus on measurable progress, maintaining flexibility and learning along the way. Celebrating small victories fosters a positive outlook and builds momentum for recovery.

Balance Decisiveness with Empathy

During a crisis, leaders are often required to make tough, quick decisions. It's vital to act swiftly, but with consideration for your team's well-being. While decisions should be informed by data, sometimes you will have to trust your gut. As a leader, you must also listen to your team's feedback.

Jon Doolen

Leadership Basics

Prompt decisions help provide direction, but empathy is key to maintaining trust. Always explain the rationale behind your decisions. When the team understands the why, they are more likely to accept the decision, even if it's difficult. If a team member refuses to follow directions and it threatens the mission or possibly makes the crisis worse, it's essential to address the issue directly and swiftly.

Here's the approach:

- **Address the Non-Compliance Immediately:** There's no room for hesitation. Clearly state the expectations and consequences. For example, "Your refusal to follow instructions is putting the entire operation at risk. This behavior is unacceptable."

- **Reinforce the Importance of the Mission:** Make it clear that the crisis is larger than any individual disagreement. "This isn't about your personal opinion. It's about the mission's success and everyone's safety."

- **Issue a Direct Order if Necessary:** If non-compliance continues, give a clear, firm directive. "You need to follow this instruction immediately. Failure to do so will result in disciplinary action."

- **Prepare for Consequences:** If the team member still refuses, you may need to follow through with disciplinary actions, up to and including suspension or termination.

Jon Doolen

Leadership Basics

Ensure the team member understands this potential outcome.

During a crisis, the well-being of the organization and mission success takes precedence. If a team member is unable to comply, you must make the difficult decision to move forward without them.

Show Up and Be Present

- **Lead by example:** Be physically and emotionally present for your team. Sometimes that means working alongside them, even when things aren't going smoothly. Your presence will reinforce your commitment and help inspire confidence.

- **Be Transparent:** Even though you may not have all the answers, being there for your team in tough moments shows that you care and are invested in their success.

Encourage Feedback and Two-Way Communication

A crisis can cause anxiety, and people often need a space to voice their concerns. Encourage open dialogue and listen actively to your team's worries. Use one-on-one check-ins and group discussions to foster communication. These should happen as often as needed to keep the mission moving forward.

Jon Doolen

Leadership Basics

This two-way interaction not only alleviates anxiety but also provides you with valuable insights that can help guide your decisions.

Empathize with Your Team's Well-Being

People are at the center of every crisis, and their mental and emotional well-being must be a priority. Offer support resources such as counseling services or flexible work arrangements, if needed. Make sure they know you're there for them, not just as a boss, but as a leader who cares about their personal well-being.

Maintaining Morale During Crisis

High morale is essential for keeping the team motivated and productive during difficult times. Here are key ways to maintain morale:

- **Celebrate Small Wins**: Recognizing achievements, no matter how small, helps people feel appreciated and motivated.

- **Remind Your Team of the Bigger Picture**: When people feel overwhelmed, they lose sight of the overall mission. By continually linking tasks to the organization's larger goals, you help them see their value and keep them focused.

- **Encourage Self-Care**: During times of stress, encourage your team to take care of themselves, mentally and physically. Promoting work-life balance and offering time off when necessary is vital for preventing burnout.

- **Work-Life Balance:** You can't pour from an empty cup. Prioritize sleep, nutrition, exercise, and downtime. A well-rested, healthy leader makes better decisions and is more effective in crisis situations. Set clear boundaries for personal time, even in busy periods. When you're at home, fully disconnect from work. During a crisis, prioritize tasks that directly impact the mission and leave less critical work for later.

Conclusion

Leading through change and crisis isn't just about managing chaos; it's about inspiring your team to push forward when everything feels uncertain. The lessons I've learned throughout my career have shown me that staying present, communicating openly, and leading with empathy are crucial to overcoming even the most difficult situations.

In every crisis, there's an opportunity, whether it's to innovate, strengthen relationships, or build resilience within your team. By maintaining a positive, focused, and transparent approach, you can guide your team through the storm, helping them see beyond the immediate challenges to the bigger picture.

Jon Doolen

Leadership Basics

As leaders, we must be willing to lead by example, stay grounded in our values, and continuously support the people who depend on us. Change and crisis will inevitably come, but with the right mindset and strategies, they can become powerful catalysts for growth and success. The key is to be adaptable, stay hopeful, and always remind your team of the purpose they're working toward.

In the end, it's not just about getting through a crisis, it's about emerging from it stronger, united, and more capable of facing whatever challenges come next.

Jon Doolen

Chapter 12: Continuous Learning and Development

In this chapter, we will explore my favorite topic of this book, the importance of lifelong learning for leaders.

In today's rapidly changing business environment, effective leadership requires continuous growth and adaptation. Leaders who prioritize lifelong learning can sharpen their skills, stay current with industry trends, and remain adaptable to change.

By investing in personal development, leaders not only enhance their own capabilities but also inspire their teams to innovate and perform at their best.

This chapter explores the importance of lifelong learning for leadership, offering actionable steps to incorporate ongoing education, mentorship, and industry awareness into your leadership journey.

Why Lifelong Learning Is Crucial for Leadership

The business landscape is constantly evolving, and as the title of Marshall Goldsmith's book accurately states, 'What Got you Here Won't Get You There.'"
To lead effectively, you must adapt to change. Leaders who prioritize continuous learning keep their skills sharp and are

better equipped to adapt to change. Lifelong learning enables leaders to stay current with new technologies, industry trends, and methodologies.

This continuous improvement sharpens your skills, enhances your decision-making ability, and equips you with a diverse set of tools to solve problems and innovate.

Effective leaders recognize that their personal development is their responsibility. While some companies offer sponsored classes or development programs, these opportunities are often limited, and few organizations do it well. Thus, leaders must actively take control of their growth.

The Benefits of Lifelong Learning

Continuous Improvement: Lifelong learning helps you refine your skills, knowledge, and competencies, ensuring you remain effective and competitive. In turn, this continuous development benefits both you and your team.

Innovation and Creativity: Exposure to new ideas and perspectives fosters creativity. Leaders who invest in learning can inspire their teams to think outside the box and tackle challenges in innovative ways.

Critical Thinking and Decision-Making: Regular learning strengthens your ability to think critically and make informed decisions. Leaders who stay well-informed can make better, data-driven choices.

Leadership Basics

Communication: Learning different communication styles improves your ability to connect with diverse teams. Effective communication is vital to reduce misunderstandings and build strong relationships with your team and stakeholders.

Self-Awareness: Lifelong learning promotes personal growth. Leaders who understand their strengths and weaknesses can relate better to others and improve their interactions with the team.

Job Satisfaction: Pursuing new skills and knowledge often leads to greater job satisfaction. As you grow, your career can become more fulfilling, and you can approach challenges from a fresh perspective.

Building Your Personal Development Plan

Creating a personal development plan (PDP) involves assessing your current skills and setting specific goals for growth. Here's how to get started:

Assess Your Current Skills: Begin by conducting a self-assessment to identify your strengths and areas for improvement. Use tools like SWOT analysis (Strengths, Weaknesses, Opportunities, and Threats), feedback from peers, and performance reviews to gather insights. This process should take time, don't rush it. You need to understand where you currently stand before planning your next steps.

Leadership Basics

Set SMART Goals: Define specific, measurable, achievable, relevant, and time-bound (SMART) goals for your personal and professional development. These goals should challenge you, but also be realistic and attainable.

Start Small: Don't overwhelm yourself with major life changes. Introduce new habits gradually, one class, one book at a time. Focus on continuous improvement rather than overhauling everything at once.

Seek Formal Education: Consider pursuing advanced degrees, certifications, or specialized courses relevant to your field. Pay special attention to any programs that offer validation or verification as a method of proving your skills versus only certifications. Anyone can memorize answers to test, not everyone can learn and then go do successfully.

Participate in networking events: Workshops, seminars, and conferences to gain new insights, expand your knowledge, and network with industry professionals.

Leadership Tip: Before spending any money on education do some research into the accreditation of the source. There are too many people offering courses and certificates that will not return on your investment.

Dedicate Time for Learning: Consistency is key to making lifelong learning a habit. Dedicate specific times in your schedule for learning activities, just like you would for meetings or other work-related tasks.

Jon Doolen

Leadership Basics

Review and Adjust: Regularly evaluate your progress and adjust your plan as needed. Lifelong learning is a dynamic process, and your goals may evolve as you gain new knowledge and insights.

Visit www.getdoolen.com and sign up for virtual training and coaching.

The Role of Mentors and Coaches

Mentorship is a crucial aspect of leadership development. A mentor or coach can provide guidance, feedback, and support as you continue your growth.

Here's how to approach this process:

Identify Potential Mentors: A mentor doesn't always have to be someone senior to you. It could be anyone in your network who possesses the expertise or skills you want to develop. Look for someone who challenges you and can provide valuable insights.

Build Rapport: Approach potential mentors with respect and clearly communicate your goals. Take time to establish a connection based on shared interests and mutual respect.

Set Clear Expectations: Make sure both you and your mentor understand the goals of the relationship. Be open to feedback and willing to take action on the advice given. Your

Leadership Basics

ability to engage in constructive dialogue with your mentor is key to the success of the relationship.

Offer Value in Return: Mentorship is a two-way relationship. Offer value to your mentor by sharing your own expertise, skills, or assistance in areas where they may need support. A mutually beneficial relationship strengthens the bond.

Informal Mentorship: Mentoring doesn't always need to follow a formal structure to be effective. Sometimes, the most valuable insights come from strategic conversations with someone who has already achieved the success you aspire to. These informal interactions - whether over a casual coffee or during a quick phone call - can offer real-world wisdom, perspective, and actionable advice.

The beauty of informal mentoring is its flexibility; you can tailor these conversations to your immediate needs and challenges. Just as in a formal program, learning from someone who has been where you want to go can accelerate your growth, providing you with lessons and guidance that textbooks or structured courses may not cover.

Staying Updated on Industry Trends

As a leader, it is crucial to stay informed about industry developments.

Here's how you can do that:

Leadership Basics

Subscribe to Industry Publications: Stay updated by subscribing to journals, magazines, and newsletters related to your field. Following thought leaders and industry experts on social media also provides valuable insights. Reach out to me on LinkedIn for help with this.

https://www.linkedin.com/in/getdoolen/

Participate in Professional Associations: Join professional organizations relevant to your industry. These groups provide resources, events, and networking opportunities. Choose your memberships wisely and ensure the groups offer tangible benefits.

Attend Conferences and Seminars: Attending industry conferences and trade shows keeps you informed about new developments and provides a platform to network with peers and gain exposure to innovative ideas.

Take Online Courses: Online learning platforms such as Coursera, edX, and LinkedIn Learning offer a wide range of courses for various fees. Invest in high-quality paid courses or choose free resources to stay updated without breaking the bank.

There are numerous free online learning options available for business professionals, offering a wide range of courses across various platforms. For instance, Harvard University provides free business courses covering topics like negotiation, leadership, and remote work.

Leadership Basics

Similarly, Coursera offers a vast selection of free courses in areas such as programming, digital marketing, and business management, many of which include certificates upon completion.

Of course, this is a great place to mention **getdoolen.com** as an online resource for leadership development and training. A much more affordable option with so many extra perks.

Engage in Networking: Attend meetups, webinars, and informal gatherings to engage with industry colleagues. Networking can lead to new opportunities and insights into the latest trends.

Conclusion

Lifelong learning is not just an option; it's a necessity for effective leadership. In a world where change is constant, those who invest in continuous development are better equipped to lead with innovation, critical thinking, and adaptability.

By prioritizing personal growth, seeking mentorship, staying updated on industry trends, and committing to self-improvement, leaders set themselves, and their teams, up for sustained success. Remember, leadership is a journey, not a destination. The more we learn, the more we grow, and the better equipped we are to navigate the challenges ahead. Embrace the process of lifelong learning and watch your leadership impact multiply.

Jon Doolen

Chapter 13: Practical Tips and Tools

In this chapter, we will dive into a toolkit of practical strategies for effective leadership. We'll explore powerful tools and strategies to help leaders assess their skills, improve time management, and manage stress effectively. Some of these tools will require a financial investment. If you're an employer, I recommend you invest in some of these for your top talent and high potential staff.

Leadership assessment tools, such as 360-degree feedback, self-assessments, and emotional intelligence evaluations, offer valuable insights into a leader's strengths, areas for growth, and potential blind spots. These tools can guide leaders in refining their styles and developing the skills necessary to lead with impact.

Additionally, mastering time management is crucial for leaders who must juggle multiple priorities. Techniques like the Eisenhower Matrix, time blocking, and the Pomodoro Technique can help leaders stay focused, organized, and productive, while also ensuring they maintain flexibility and approachability with their teams.

Finally, stress management is an often overlooked but critical component of leadership. Leaders who practice mindfulness, prioritize work-life balance, and maintain strong support systems can effectively manage stress, stay energized, and perform at their best.

By leveraging these tools and strategies, leaders can foster both personal growth and organizational success.

Leadership Assessment Tools

There are many tools available to assess and improve your leadership skills. These assessments can help you gain insights into your leadership style, strengths, and areas for improvement.

Here are some tools that I recommend:

360-Degree Feedback: This is a comprehensive process where leaders receive anonymous feedback from peers, subordinates, and supervisors. It provides a well-rounded view of your leadership effectiveness. For this tool to be useful, it's essential to ensure honesty and fairness in the feedback process. Developing an action plan based on this feedback, with the help of a qualified professional, can help you grow and improve.

Self-Assessment Questionnaires: These allow leaders to evaluate their own behaviors and leadership styles. Tools like the Leadership Practices Inventory (LPI) or Myers-Briggs Type Indicator (MBTI) offer valuable insights into how you approach leadership and how you can refine your style.

StrengthsFinder: This tool identifies your top strengths and talents, which can be leveraged to maximize your leadership impact. However, be cautious not to over-develop these strengths to the point where they become liabilities. Keep track of your growth with measurable outcomes.

Emotional Intelligence (EI) Assessments: Emotional intelligence is often underestimated, but it's a crucial skill for leaders. Tools like the Emotional Intelligence Appraisal or EQ-i 2.0 measure your self-awareness, empathy, and social skills, helping you enhance your emotional intelligence and improve your leadership capacity.

Time Management Techniques

Time management is an area where almost everyone struggles. While there is no perfect method, there are several strategies that can help leaders maximize their productivity and stay focused on what matters most:

The Eisenhower Matrix: This tool helps prioritize tasks based on urgency and importance. (Citation 17)

The matrix divides tasks into four quadrants:

- **Urgent and Important**: Handle these immediately.
- **Important but Not Urgent**: Schedule time for these to prevent future crises.
- **Urgent but Not Important**: Delegate these tasks if possible.
- **Neither Urgent nor Important**: Eliminate or minimize these tasks.

Leadership Basics

Here is a visual representation of the Eisenhower Matrix. It organizes tasks into four quadrants based on their urgency and importance:

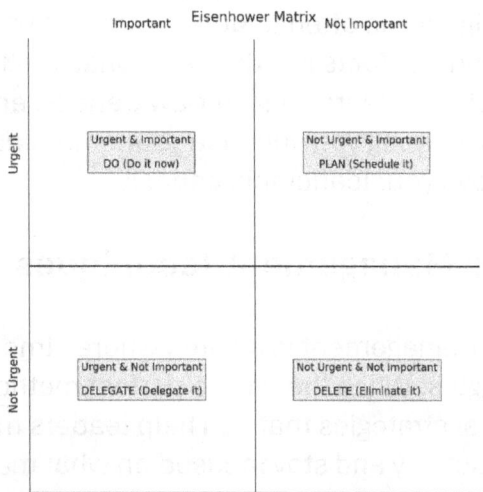

Time Blocking: Dedicate specific blocks of time for focused work, meetings, and breaks. Blocking your calendar this way helps prevent distractions and ensures that high-priority tasks receive the attention they deserve.

Leadership Tip: Time blocking can boost productivity, but over-scheduling can make you unapproachable and inflexible.

Here's how to strike the right balance:

- **Prioritize Critical Tasks**: Block time for high-impact responsibilities first, but leave gaps for flexibility and

Leadership Basics

> unexpected needs. Leadership is about being available when your team needs you.
> - **Set 'Office Hours'**: Dedicate specific blocks where your team knows you're open for questions or collaboration. This keeps you accessible without derailing your focus.
> - **Avoid Back-to-Back Blocks**: Leave buffer time between tasks to catch your breath, recalibrate, or handle quick team concerns.
> - **Audit Your Calendar Weekly**: Evaluate if your blocks reflect your priorities and allow time for leadership duties like mentoring, problem-solving, and strategy.

Time blocking is a tool, not a cage. Use it to create space for focus while staying approachable as a leader.

Pomodoro Technique: This technique helps boost focus by using timed intervals. Work for 25 minutes (one Pomodoro), then take a 5-minute break. After four Pomodoros, take a longer break (15-30 minutes). This method is especially effective for maintaining concentration and avoiding burnout. (Citation 18)

Prioritization by Value: Instead of focusing solely on urgent tasks, assess tasks based on their value and impact on your goals. This method ensures that you invest your energy in activities that drive significant results.

Delegation: Delegation is one of the most important skills a leader can have. Assign responsibilities to team members based on their strengths and capacity. Delegation not only frees up your time but also empowers your team and builds trust.

Stress Management Strategies

Managing stress is a critical aspect of leadership. Leaders must stay mentally and physically fit to perform at their best.

Here are some practical strategies to help manage stress:

Mindfulness and Meditation: Taking time to focus on the present moment can reduce stress and improve clarity. Apps like Headspace or Calm can guide you through mindfulness exercises. Set aside time each day for these practices to stay calm and centered.

Exercise: Regular physical activity helps reduce stress and boosts overall well-being. Aim for at least 30 minutes of moderate exercise most days of the week. Exercise has proven benefits for improving mood, enhancing focus, and reducing anxiety.

Effective Time Management: As mentioned, using time management techniques like time blocking or the Eisenhower Matrix can help you stay on top of your tasks, reducing stress and preventing last-minute rushes.

Work-Life Balance: Defining a healthy work-life balance is essential to avoid burnout. Set clear boundaries between work and personal life. Regularly schedule time for activities that bring you joy, whether it's spending time with family, pursuing hobbies, or relaxing.

Support Systems: Having a strong support network, whether it's family, friends, or colleagues, can be invaluable. These relationships provide emotional support and practical help when you need it most.

Professional Help: If stress becomes overwhelming, don't hesitate to seek professional help. Many organizations offer employee assistance programs (EAPs) that provide access to counselors or therapists. There's no shame in asking for help, and it can significantly improve your mental health and effectiveness as a leader.

Conclusion

In today's fast-paced, ever-evolving work environment, great leadership demands more than just strategic thinking or technical expertise. By utilizing leadership assessment tools, leaders can gain valuable insights into their strengths and areas for improvement, providing a solid foundation for growth.

Time management strategies such as the Eisenhower Matrix, time blocking, and the Pomodoro Technique empower leaders to focus on what matters most, ensuring productivity without sacrificing flexibility or approachability.

Leadership Basics

Equally important is the ability to manage stress effectively. A well-balanced leader who practices mindfulness, stays physically active, and maintains strong support systems is better equipped to navigate challenges, make sound decisions, and inspire their teams.

Ultimately, becoming an exceptional leader is a journey of continuous learning and self-improvement. By incorporating these tools and strategies into your daily routine, you can strengthen your leadership effectiveness, foster a positive work environment, and achieve long-term success - for both yourself and your team.

Leadership Basics

Chapter 14: Let's discuss the role faith plays in Leadership

In this chapter, I explore how faith, or spirituality, can intersect with leadership and the workplace. Faith has profoundly influenced leadership throughout history, serving as a moral compass, a source of resilience, and a guide for building community and fostering purpose.

This chapter explores the interplay between faith and leadership, examining how belief systems have shaped ethical decision-making, inspired social movements, and provided strength during crises. It also delves into the distinction between faith and religion, offering insights on integrating personal values into leadership without imposing them on others.

With practical advice and real-life examples, this chapter highlights how faith-based principles can guide leaders to act with integrity, authenticity, and respect in both their personal and professional lives.

The History of Faith in Leadership

Faith has played a significant role in leadership throughout history, shaping the principles, decisions, and actions of leaders across cultures and time periods.
Here's a look at its influence:

Jon Doolen

Leadership Basics

Foundation of Ethical Leadership: Faith has often served as a moral compass, guiding leaders in making ethical decisions. Many historic leaders, from religious figures like Mahatma Gandhi to U.S. presidents like Abraham Lincoln, leaned on their faith to promote justice, compassion, and integrity.

Inspiring Vision and Purpose: Leaders with a foundation in faith often draw on their beliefs to inspire a higher purpose. Faith has fueled movements like the civil rights movement, with Martin Luther King Jr.'s leadership rooted in his Christian faith, calling for equality and nonviolence.

Resilience in Crisis: Faith provides leaders with inner strength to face adversity. During moments of war, economic turmoil, or personal challenges, leaders like Winston Churchill and Nelson Mandela relied on their faith to maintain hope and perseverance.

Building Community and Unity: Faith has historically been a unifying force, encouraging leaders to foster inclusivity and collaboration. Religious or spiritual communities have often formed the backbone of collective action, from building nations to aiding humanitarian efforts.

Shaping Laws and Governance: Many legal and governance systems worldwide have been influenced by faith traditions. Leaders historically used faith to create laws based on principles of fairness, accountability, and care for the vulnerable.

Navigating Controversy and Conflict: While faith has inspired great leadership, it has also been a point of contention. Some leaders have used faith divisively, while others have worked to reconcile differences, exemplifying leadership that bridges divides.

Modern Leadership with Faith: In today's diverse world, faith in leadership often takes a more inclusive approach. Leaders draw on their values without imposing them, modeling respect for varied beliefs while staying true to their own convictions.

The Role of Faith in Leadership Today

Faith in leadership doesn't mean you need to preach or push your beliefs on others. It's about being authentic and aligning your values with how you lead and interact with others. For me, faith means believing in doing the right thing, showing respect for others, and striving to be a better person each day. It's about staying true to your core values, regardless of external challenges or the actions of others.

The terms **faith** and **religion** are often used interchangeably, but they represent distinct concepts.
Faith

- **Definition**: Faith is a deeply personal trust, belief, or confidence in something or someone, often without requiring proof. It can relate to spirituality, values, or even trust in people or principles.

- **Individual**: Faith is inherently personal and subjective. It's about one's internal relationship with beliefs, whether in a higher power, humanity, or a guiding principle.

Leadership Basics

- **Broad Application**: Faith is not limited to religious contexts. For example, you can have faith in love, in the goodness of humanity, or in a mission or cause.

- **Emotional Connection**: Faith is often rooted in feelings of hope, trust, and purpose, and it doesn't necessarily rely on structure or formal practices.

Religion

- **Definition**: Religion is a structured system of beliefs, practices, and rituals centered around a higher power, deity, or ultimate truth. It often includes shared doctrines, sacred texts, and organized communities.

- **Organized**: Religion is typically communal, offering a set of rules, teachings, and traditions that guide its followers.

- **Institutional**: It is often tied to formal organizations, such as churches, mosques, temples, or synagogues, with leadership and hierarchical systems.

- **Cultural Aspect**: Religion often intertwines with culture, shaping traditions, holidays, and social norms.

Leadership Basics

Key Differences

Scope: Faith is broader and personal, while religion is specific and institutional.

Structure: Faith doesn't require formal practices or a community; religion provides a framework of rituals, teachings, and community worship.

Focus: Faith is about belief and trust; religion is about organized worship and adherence to a set of principles or dogma.

Inclusivity: Faith can exist without religion (e.g., someone spiritual but not religious), but religion often assumes faith in its beliefs.

How They Connect

Faith can exist independently of religion, but religion often helps nurture and organize faith. For example, someone might have faith in God (personal belief) and express that faith through Christianity or Judaism (religion). Alternatively, someone might have faith in humanity or the universe without subscribing to any religious system.

In short, **faith is the seed; religion is the garden where some choose to nurture it.**

I don't like labels and try to avoid them when I can. I prefer to

Leadership Basics

describe myself as "faith-based," but I do recognize that labels can sometimes be helpful.

So, I'll say that I'm a Christian, specifically a Methodist. I truly believe that faith plays a major role in shaping who I am as a leader. I'm not perfect; I use profanity at times, and I'm not proud of it. I lose my temper, and I have moments that don't reflect my faith, but I'm a work in progress.

My faith does not provide an excuse for bad behavior.

My faith provides direction, stability, and a sense of purpose, whether in personal challenges or leadership decisions. I've seen firsthand how it has guided me through key moments in my life, from overcoming personal struggles to making career choices.

One pivotal moment came in 2016 when my faith led me to move my family from Omaha, Nebraska, to Detroit, Michigan. Despite achieving success professionally and within my team, I felt something was missing.

I prayed for a change.

What was missing was personal fulfillment. My family found the right school district, neighborhood, and church community that fit us perfectly. This new support system has helped us thrive, so much so, that today, my wife and I are both self-employed entrepreneurs who are present for our kids during the important moments of their lives and development.

Jon Doolen

Merging Faith and Leadership

One of the most challenging aspects of integrating faith into leadership is the desire to remain authentic while respecting others' beliefs. For some, this might be a non-issue, but for others, there can be fear of judgment or misunderstanding.

Over the years, I've come to realize that it's not only okay to be open about faith, it's crucial. But, just as important, it's equally necessary to respect others' viewpoints and not impose our own beliefs on them.

Doing it "right" means being a leader who shows kindness, integrity, and authenticity. If you express your faith in the workplace, do so by modeling positive behaviors and ethical actions that align with your values, not just through words. Leading with integrity and treating others with respect should be the hallmark of any faith-based leadership approach.

Faith-Friendly Workplaces

There has been a notable shift toward acknowledging faith in the workplace in recent years. Companies are beginning to recognize the importance of respecting diverse religious and spiritual beliefs. Below are some of the emerging trends around faith-friendly workplaces:

Religious Diversity and Inclusion: More organizations are expanding their diversity and inclusion efforts to include faith-based diversity. This may involve creating spaces for dialogue about religious beliefs or offering flexible policies for religious holidays.

Spiritual Wellness Initiatives: Some organizations are embracing the connection between spirituality and employee well-being. These initiatives may include offering meditation spaces, spiritual coaching, or designated prayer rooms for employees to practice their faith during work hours.

Employee Resource Groups (ERGs) for Faith: Certain companies are supporting Faith-Based Employee Resource Groups (ERGs), which provide a platform for employees to connect with others who share their spiritual values. These groups create safe spaces where employees can express their beliefs without fear of judgment.

Mindfulness and Meditation: While not inherently religious, mindfulness practices rooted in spiritual traditions have become increasingly popular in workplaces. These practices help reduce stress, enhance focus, and foster productivity, making them a valuable tool in any organization.

Ethical Leadership: Many companies are aligning their corporate values with broader ethical principles found in faith traditions, such as compassion, service, and integrity. This type of leadership focuses on doing the right thing, even when it's hard, and creating a workplace that prioritizes fairness and responsibility.

Leadership Basics

The Intersection of Faith, Leadership, and Organizational Culture

As companies begin to embrace spirituality and faith in the workplace, it's essential to create an inclusive culture where employees feel respected for their individual beliefs. Organizations that respect religious and spiritual diversity help foster an environment of trust and respect. This encourages employees to bring their whole selves to work, which can lead to higher levels of engagement, creativity, and innovation.

Leaders who promote faith-friendly workplaces understand that spirituality isn't confined to organized religion but encompasses a broader understanding of the individual's need for purpose, connection, and well-being. They support an environment where employees feel safe to explore their spirituality, express their beliefs, and engage in conversations about how their faith informs their work and life.

Leading with Faith and Integrity

Being a leader with faith doesn't mean you have to make a grand public display of your beliefs. It's about living in a way that aligns with your values, treating others with kindness and respect, and always striving to make ethical decisions. Your faith can be a source of guidance and strength as you navigate the complexities of leadership.

As I've learned, integrating faith into leadership is a personal

Jon Doolen

Leadership Basics

journey, but it's one that can bring tremendous value to both your professional life and the lives of those you lead. It's about doing the right thing, not because you expect anything in return, but because it aligns with who you are at your core.

If you're a leader, don't be afraid to bring your faith into your leadership style, but always do it with authenticity, respect, and integrity. Treat people right, stay true to your values, and lead with compassion. This approach will not only help you grow as a leader but will inspire others to do the same.

I have had many experiences over my years where I trusted a co-worker with perspective on my faith and they did not agree and attempted to sway my beliefs or apply bully type of attention to belittle what I believe.

Here's how to lead yourself - and others - through these situations with integrity:

Know Your Core Values: Be clear on what you believe and why. When you're rooted in your values, others' attempts to sway or belittle you lose their power. Self-determination starts with confidence in who you are.

Set Boundaries with Respect: If a conversation turns confrontational or dismissive, calmly assert, "I respect your perspective, but I ask for the same in return." Boundaries protect both your beliefs and your professional relationships.

Respond, Don't React: Resist the urge to retaliate or escalate. Instead, demonstrate grace by listening without compromising

Jon Doolen

Leadership Basics

your stance. Faith is often best exemplified by your actions, not debates.

Find Supportive Allies: Surround yourself with co-workers or mentors who respect and uplift your values, even if they don't share them. Their support reinforces your resolve.

Lead by Example: When others see your unwavering belief paired with kindness and professionalism, it speaks louder than words. Inspire respect by embodying humility and strength.

Faith and self-determination are deeply personal, yet your leadership in these moments can leave a lasting, positive impression on others, even those who may disagree.

Faith and leadership can coexist in the corporate world, even when confronted by someone who is atheist or does not share the same belief system. It's essential to navigate these relationships with respect and empathy, acknowledging that everyone brings their own worldview to the table. While it's important to uphold your own beliefs and values, the key is to create a space where differences are respected and dialogue remains constructive.

Consider focusing on universal principles like integrity, accountability, and collaboration that transcend religious beliefs, allowing you to foster a work environment grounded in mutual respect. Lead by example, showing that your faith shapes your character and decision-making, while avoiding the imposition of your views on others. In doing so, you can build a rapport based on shared values without compromising who you are. Encourage open conversations, actively listen, and remain open-minded, understanding that fostering an inclusive environment is a two-way street where both your beliefs and the other person's perspective can coexist peacefully.

Using your faith ethically in business means aligning your actions with your beliefs, even when the pressure to make compromises arises. I've worked with companies where faith was openly referenced during the interview process, and it was a topic often discussed in business meetings. However, over time, it became clear that their actions did not reflect the values they claimed to uphold. Decisions were made, and people were treated in ways that were inconsistent with the faith-based principles they professed.

This disconnect inevitably comes to light, though your business partners and teammates may not confront you directly, they notice. Conversations happen behind closed doors, and your integrity begins to erode in their eyes.

The truth is, behavior will always speak louder than words, and when actions don't align with beliefs, your reputation suffers, no matter how well you project your values in the beginning. Integrity is key, and it's vital to ensure your actions consistently mirror the principles you stand for.

Conclusion

Faith has been an enduring force in leadership, providing guidance, strength, and a foundation for ethical decision-making throughout history. From shaping laws and governance to

Leadership Basics

inspiring social change, faith's influence extends beyond individual beliefs to impact entire communities and organizations.

As leaders, the challenge lies in integrating faith authentically, respecting diverse perspectives, and leading with integrity.

In today's increasingly diverse and inclusive workplace, the role of faith in leadership has evolved to focus on shared values such as compassion, resilience, and purpose. By leading through actions that align with core principles, leaders can inspire trust and respect while fostering a culture of mutual understanding.

Ultimately, faith in leadership is not about imposing beliefs but about living them. It's about showing kindness, making decisions with integrity, and treating others with respect, qualities that transcend religious affiliations and unite people around common goals.

When leaders embody these principles, they create a legacy not just of success, but of meaning and purpose that leaves a lasting, positive impact on those they serve.

Jon Doolen

Leadership Basics

Chapter 15: The Future of Leadership

In this chapter, we explore the emerging trends shaping leadership today. While leadership principles remain largely unchanged at their core, new challenges arise due to technological advancements, shifting workforce dynamics, and evolving societal expectations.

The landscape of leadership is rapidly evolving, shaped by new challenges and opportunities in our increasingly complex world. As businesses adapt to technological advances, shifting work models, and changing societal expectations, leaders must remain agile and forward-thinking.

Leaders today are not just tasked with driving profitability; they are also responsible for fostering innovation, promoting inclusivity, and integrating purpose-driven goals that align with broader societal values. From mastering new technologies and navigating hybrid work environments to championing DEI initiatives and advocating for sustainable practices, effective leadership requires a blend of technical expertise, emotional intelligence, and a commitment to continuous learning.

The ability to adapt, collaborate, and communicate effectively in an increasingly digital and socially conscious world will define the leaders of tomorrow.

Jon Doolen

Leadership Basics

Emerging Trends in Leadership

Digital Transformation and Technology Integration

As businesses become increasingly digital, leaders must harness the power of digital tools, data analytics, and artificial intelligence (AI) to drive efficiency and foster innovation. Understanding these technologies is not only crucial for growth but also for safeguarding organizations from potential threats like cybersecurity risks. Leaders who can embrace and guide digital transformation will position themselves, and their teams, on the cutting edge.

Here's how to lead effectively in this space:

Start with a Vision: Clearly define how technology will support your organization's mission. Ensure your team understands *why* these changes matter and how they'll benefit the business and their roles.

Upskill Your Team: Invest in training so everyone feels confident using digital tools. A well-equipped team can turn new technologies into opportunities for innovation rather than sources of frustration.

Adopt Incrementally: Don't overwhelm your team with too much change at once. Introduce new tools and processes in phases, and gather feedback to ensure successful integration.

Jon Doolen

Leadership Basics

Prioritize Cybersecurity: Lead by example in recognizing the importance of safeguarding data. Make cybersecurity a proactive part of your digital strategy, not an afterthought.

Use Data to Drive Decisions: Leverage analytics to make informed decisions, but balance this with human insight. Encourage your team to blend data-driven strategies with creativity and critical thinking.

Digital transformation isn't just a technical upgrade, it's a leadership opportunity. By guiding your team with clarity and care, you'll ensure technology becomes a tool for progress, not a barrier to it.

Remote and Hybrid Work

The COVID-19 pandemic accelerated the shift towards remote and hybrid work models, and even as the world emerges from the crisis, the debate continues. Some companies embrace these flexible working arrangements, recognizing the benefits of employee autonomy and work-life balance. Others, however, are pulling back, believing that in-office collaboration is key to innovation and productivity.

As a leader, balancing in-office and remote work, and understanding which employees thrive in which environment, will be crucial for maintaining productivity, engagement, and talent retention. If you are a leader making the decision to bring your team back to the office, be transparent in your reasoning, "because I said so" is a fair answer, after all, you're the boss. Just be honest about it.

Leadership Basics

Here's how to lead effectively in this evolving workplace dynamic:

Communicate the "Why" Clearly: If you're requiring in-office work, explain the reasoning with honesty and context. Transparency builds trust, even if the decision isn't popular. Avoid vague mandates -connect the decision to team goals, collaboration needs, or long-term strategy.

Focus on Outcomes, Not Location: Whether remote or in-office, prioritize results over physical presence. Set clear goals and performance metrics so everyone knows what success looks like, regardless of where they work.

Adapt to Individual Needs: Some employees thrive remotely, while others perform better in the office. Pay attention to individual preferences and strengths, and, when possible, provide flexibility to foster productivity and engagement.

Preserve Team Connection: Hybrid models can strain collaboration and culture. Invest in regular team check-ins, clear communication channels, and occasional in-person gatherings to keep relationships strong.

Be Open to Feedback: Decisions about work models are rarely one-size-fits-all. Regularly gather feedback to assess how your approach is impacting productivity and morale and be willing to adjust as needed.

Jon Doolen

Leadership Basics

Balancing flexibility with structure is the key to thriving in remote and hybrid environments. By focusing on communication, fairness, and adaptability, you'll create a team culture that works effectively no matter where "work" happens.

Diversity, Equity, and Inclusion (DEI)

Diversity, Equity, and Inclusion (DEI) is a hot-button issue that is often politicized, but its value in creating positive, innovative workplaces cannot be ignored. DEI initiatives seek to create environments where all individuals feel respected, valued, and supported, regardless of their background. Leaders must champion these initiatives, ensuring they create inclusive cultures while promoting merit-based advancement and productivity. Navigating DEI requires a commitment to understanding diverse perspectives and fostering equitable opportunities for all employees.

DEI programs often falter when they prioritize filling roles based solely on DEI metrics rather than merit, leading to unintended consequences for both individuals and organizations. Many companies have begun scaling back these initiatives, not because the concept is flawed, but because they failed to provide the necessary support, training, and mentorship to the DEI candidates placed in high-priority roles.

The individuals in these positions did not fail; it was leadership that fell short, by neglecting to equip their teams with the tools and guidance needed to succeed. Effective DEI programs must balance representation with competency and commit to fostering an environment where diverse talent is not only welcomed but empowered to thrive.

When done right, DEI can elevate performance and innovation, but it requires accountability and a long-term investment in development to truly succeed.
Everyone has an obligation to develop themselves and participate in corporate sponsored development.

Here's how to apply DEI effectively:

Balance Representation and Competency: While diverse hiring is essential, it's equally important to ensure that all employees, regardless of their background, are equipped with the skills and support they need to succeed. Prioritize both diverse representation *and* the development of competencies to ensure long-term success.

Invest in Training and Mentorship: Don't just focus on placing individuals in diverse roles. Provide ongoing training, mentorship, and development opportunities to help them excel. Effective DEI programs include continuous support and resources, ensuring all talent is given the chance to thrive, regardless of their starting point.

Accountability for Everyone: DEI isn't just the responsibility of one group or department, it's a collective effort. Hold everyone accountable, from senior leaders to individual contributors, for fostering an inclusive environment. This includes promoting merit-based advancement and equitable opportunities for growth.

Focus on Empowerment, Not Just Representation: DEI initiatives should focus on creating an environment where employees feel respected, valued, and supported in reaching their full potential. Encourage and provide opportunities for all team members to develop and advance, ensuring that merit and skill are at the core of decision-making.

Lead with Empathy and Understanding: To champion DEI, leaders must actively listen to diverse perspectives and acknowledge the unique challenges that individuals from underrepresented groups may face. Cultivate a culture where these voices are heard, respected, and prioritized in the decision-making process.

Effective DEI isn't about filling quotas, it's about creating an environment where everyone has the tools, resources, and support to succeed.

By investing in the development of all employees and holding the organization accountable for fostering inclusion, leaders can drive performance, innovation, and lasting change.

Leadership Basics

Sustainability and Social Responsibility

More businesses are recognizing the importance of sustainability, both environmental and social. Leaders are expected to integrate responsible practices into their strategies and decision-making, aligning their values with those of their employees and customers. However, it's crucial to approach sustainability with integrity.

Leaders must educate themselves about ethical, sustainable practices and not succumb to societal pressures if the resources to make genuine change aren't available.

Here's how to lead responsibly in this area:

Educate Yourself and Your Team: Take the time to understand what sustainable practices truly mean for your industry. Avoid "greenwashing" (superficial claims of sustainability) by investing in the knowledge needed to make informed decisions.

Start Small, Stay Authentic: If resources for large-scale sustainability initiatives aren't available, begin with practical, incremental changes that align with your organization's values. Focus on actions that are meaningful and measurable rather than grand gestures that lack substance.

Align Values with Actions: Ensure your sustainability efforts reflect your company's mission and resonate with

Jon Doolen

Leadership Basics

employees and customers. Authenticity is key—empty promises can damage trust and credibility.

Engage Stakeholders: Collaborate with employees, customers, and partners to identify meaningful ways to implement sustainable practices. This fosters a shared sense of purpose and accountability.

Communicate Transparently: Be honest about what your organization can and cannot achieve in terms of sustainability. Share your goals, progress, and challenges openly to build trust and credibility.

Measure Impact, Not Intentions: Track the results of your initiatives and adjust as needed. Sustainability isn't just about effort; it's about real-world impact.

By focusing on authentic, achievable steps toward sustainability, you'll demonstrate integrity while building trust with your employees, customers, and community. True leadership in sustainability is about progress, not perfection.

Agility and Resilience in the Face of Change

The speed at which change occurs today can feel overwhelming. However, change for the sake of change is unnecessary; leaders should promote change that leads to growth and advancement.

An attitude of continuous improvement, always being ready for the next opportunity, and embracing learning is essential.

Jon Doolen

Leadership Basics

Leaders who prioritize agility, resilience, and adaptability will ensure their organizations are equipped to pivot quickly when necessary.

Here's how to lead through constant change:

Champion Continuous Learning: Encourage your team to see learning as a journey, not a destination. Offer opportunities for skill development, cross-training, and innovation. This prepares them to embrace change with confidence.

Promote Agility and Resilience: Teach your team to remain adaptable in the face of uncertainty. Foster a mindset where challenges are seen as opportunities for growth, not setbacks. Encourage flexibility, where people are ready to pivot when needed.

Focus on Purposeful Change: Ensure any change introduced is aligned with the organization's strategic goals. Before implementing change, ask: "How does this support growth?" Prioritize initiatives that will drive forward-thinking progress.

Lead by Example: Be the first to demonstrate agility and adaptability in your own work. Show your team how you handle change - your actions will set the tone for how they respond.

Create a Safe Environment for Experimentation: Encourage calculated risk-taking. Allow your team to try new

Jon Doolen

things, fail fast, and learn quickly without fear of negative consequences.

Celebrate Small Wins: Every time your team successfully adapts or learns something new, recognize and celebrate it. These small victories create momentum and reinforce the idea that change is a chance for improvement.

By fostering a culture where continuous improvement is valued, your organization will be equipped to navigate change effectively, ensuring long-term growth and resilience.

Soft Skills: From "Soft" to "Power" Skills

In the past, "soft skills" like communication, emotional intelligence, and empathy were often viewed as secondary to technical expertise. Today, these skills are more valuable than ever and are now being referred to as "power skills" or "core skills." Effective communication is one of the most important of these skills.

Mastering communication, particularly within diverse teams, is crucial for success. Leaders who focus on developing these people skills, along with their technical expertise, will thrive in today's workplace.

Here's how you can enhance your ability to connect with your team and lead effectively:

Leadership Basics

Invest in Active Listening: Effective communication isn't just about speaking clearly, it's about listening well. Practice active listening by giving your full attention, asking clarifying questions, and validating others' perspectives. This creates trust and ensures you understand your team's needs and concerns.

Foster Open Dialogue: Encourage a culture of openness where team members feel safe sharing their ideas, concerns, and feedback. Create regular touchpoints for informal conversations, not just formal meetings, so your team knows you value their input.

Adapt Your Communication Style: Different people respond to different communication styles. Be aware of how your team members prefer to communicate - whether it's through direct conversations, emails, or more visual methods - and adjust accordingly to make sure your message is understood.

Develop Emotional Intelligence: Work on understanding and managing your own emotions, as well as recognizing and responding to the emotions of others. This skill helps you navigate challenging conversations, motivate your team, and resolve conflicts in a productive way.

Empathy is Key: Take the time to understand your team's challenges, both personally and professionally. Showing genuine care and concern builds loyalty and helps people feel supported, especially during tough times.

Leadership Basics

Give Constructive Feedback: Provide feedback that's clear, actionable, and framed positively. Focus on development rather than criticism, and always acknowledge strengths before suggesting areas for improvement.

Encourage Collaboration: People skills aren't just about managing relationships, they're about creating environments where people can collaborate effectively. Foster teamwork by facilitating conversations, encouraging knowledge-sharing, and leading by example in collaboration.

Leaders who develop strong communication and emotional intelligence will not only build stronger relationships within their teams but also lead with greater influence and effectiveness in today's diverse, fast-changing workplace.

Continuous Learning

The best leaders commit to lifelong learning. With new platforms, courses, and certifications emerging all the time, leaders must find learning opportunities that fit their styles and keep them up to date with industry trends, technological advancements, and best practices.

Leaders who consistently seek to enhance their knowledge and skills will remain relevant in an ever-changing landscape.

Here's how you can incorporate learning into your leadership journey:

Jon Doolen

Leadership Basics

Schedule Regular Learning Time: Just as you schedule meetings and tasks, make time for learning. Block out time each week to read industry articles, take courses, or attend webinars. Consistent, bite-sized learning adds up over time.

Focus on Practical Application: Don't just learn for the sake of learning. apply new knowledge to your daily leadership practices. Whether it's a new tool, a leadership technique, or an industry trend, implement it and see how it impacts your team or business.

Curate Learning Resources: With endless options available, be selective about where you invest your time. Follow thought leaders, subscribe to industry journals, and choose courses or certifications that align with your current challenges and future goals.

Learn from Others: Seek out mentors, network with peers, and engage in discussions with your team. Learning isn't just about formal education, it's about hearing different perspectives and gaining insights from the experiences of others.

Stay Agile: The best leaders understand that learning isn't just about accumulating knowledge, it's about adaptability. Stay open to new ideas and be ready to shift your approach when new information or innovations present themselves.

Lead by Example: Show your team that learning is a priority by actively pursuing growth opportunities. Encourage them

Leadership Basics

to do the same by providing resources, recommending courses, and creating a culture of continuous improvement.

By making learning a consistent habit, you not only expand your own capabilities but also inspire your team to embrace growth and stay ahead of the curve. The most effective leaders aren't just experts, they're always evolving.

The Digital Literacy Imperative

Leaders today need to be digitally literate, capable of engaging in conversations about data analytics, AI, and digital tools. Even if they are not the technical experts, leaders must understand these concepts well enough to guide their teams, drive innovation, and make informed decisions.

Here's how you can integrate it into your leadership approach:

Invest Time in Learning the Basics: You don't need to be a data scientist or AI specialist, but having a solid understanding of key concepts like data analytics, AI, and digital tools is crucial. Start by taking online courses or reading articles that explain these topics in simple terms.

Ask the Right Questions: When discussing digital tools or data, focus on understanding how these elements can drive growth, innovation, and efficiency. Ask your team or experts in the field to explain how technology impacts your business strategy, and make sure you're clear on the implications of those technologies.

Promote Digital Fluency Across Your Team: Encourage your team to become digitally literate as well. Foster a culture where they feel empowered to engage with new technologies, ask questions, and explore tools that can improve productivity and decision-making.

Leverage Technology to Make Informed Decisions: Use data and analytics to guide your decision-making. Even if you're not the one crunching the numbers, ensure you're familiar with the tools that provide insights and learn how to interpret them. This will help you make informed, data-driven decisions.

Collaborate with Tech Experts: Build a strong network with IT professionals or digital experts who can guide you when necessary. Regularly seek their input on strategic decisions and stay updated on the latest tech trends that could impact your business.

Stay Agile and Curious: The digital landscape is always evolving. Be open to learning new digital tools and technologies, and remain flexible in adopting innovations that can enhance your leadership capabilities and business performance.

By becoming digitally literate, you'll not only lead with confidence but also inspire your team to embrace digital transformation and stay ahead of the curve.

Leadership Basics

Adaptable and Inclusive Leadership Styles

Traditional command-and-control leadership styles are giving way to more collaborative, participative approaches. Involving team members in decision-making, valuing their input, and fostering an environment that supports experimentation and flexibility will help leaders cultivate innovative, resilient teams.

Leaders should also be aware of the shifting workplace structure, from hierarchical to more networked, decentralized teams. Empowering teams to take ownership of their work will foster a sense of accountability and drive.

Here's how to apply this in your leadership:

Involve Your Team in Decision-Making: Don't just dictate decisions, invite your team into the conversation. Ask for their perspectives, ideas, and feedback. By involving them in decisions, you build trust, increase engagement, and foster a sense of ownership over the outcomes.

Foster a Culture of Experimentation: Encourage a mindset of experimentation and learning. Create an environment where it's safe to try new things, make mistakes, and learn from them. Innovation often comes from trying something different and iterating based on feedback.

Empower Teams to Take Ownership: Instead of micromanaging, give your team autonomy to make decisions within their scope. Encourage them to take

Leadership Basics

responsibility for their work and hold themselves accountable for results. When people feel a sense of ownership, they're more motivated and committed to the success of the team.

Be Flexible in Your Approach: The days of rigid hierarchies are fading. Embrace flexibility in how your team works, collaborates, and solves problems. Foster a networked structure where information flows freely and people can work across silos to get things done.

Lead as a Facilitator, Not a Director: Shift from traditional command-and-control to being a facilitator who provides guidance, removes obstacles, and empowers your team to take initiative. Support their development by coaching them and helping them grow, rather than always telling them what to do.

Celebrate Collaboration and Collective Success: Acknowledge when teams come together to solve problems or innovate. Celebrate group accomplishments, which reinforces the importance of teamwork and collaboration in achieving business goals.

By adopting a more participative, collaborative leadership style, you'll create an environment where your team feels empowered, accountable, and motivated to contribute to the organization's success.

Jon Doolen

Leadership Basics

Treat Them Like Partners

Great leaders understand the value of treating their team members like business partners rather than just direct reports. This approach fosters mutual respect, encourages accountability, and empowers individuals to take ownership of their decisions as if they were stakeholders in the organization's success.

James, who reported to me for years, once shared that the reason he stayed was because I never treated him like an employee but always like a partner. His input was valued, his contributions were recognized, and he was held accountable for outcomes as if they were his own.

This mindset creates a culture where people are more engaged, invested, and inspired to go beyond expectations because they feel truly part of the mission. When leaders build partnerships within their teams, they not only strengthen relationships but also unlock the collective potential needed to achieve extraordinary results.

Here's how to apply this approach in your leadership:

Value Their Input: Just as you would consult a business partner, actively seek input from your team members. Make them feel that their opinions matter by listening attentively and incorporating their ideas when making decisions.

Empower Accountability: Hold your team accountable as if they were stakeholders in the success of the business.

Jon Doolen

Leadership Basics

Encourage them to take ownership of their projects and outcomes. This sense of responsibility will motivate them to perform at a higher level because they understand that their contributions directly impact the company's success.

Recognize and Appreciate Contributions: Acknowledge the hard work and achievements of your team members. Regularly express gratitude for their efforts and highlight how their contributions are essential to the overall mission. Recognition reinforces the value they bring to the table.

Promote Shared Goals and Vision: Make sure your team understands the larger mission and vision of the organization. When everyone is aligned and working towards common goals, they will be more motivated and invested in the company's success.

Foster a Collaborative Environment: Encourage collaboration and cross-functional teamwork. Just as partners in a business collaborate to reach shared objectives, facilitate opportunities for your team to work together and build strong, mutually supportive relationships.

Be Transparent and Honest: Treat your team as trusted partners by being open about business challenges and opportunities. Transparency breeds trust and makes employees feel like they're part of the solution, rather than just executing orders.

Invest in Their Growth: Show that you care about their personal and professional development. Like a business

Jon Doolen

partner, invest in their success and provide opportunities for growth, mentorship, and learning. When they feel supported, they'll invest even more in the business's success.

By treating your team as business partners, you're not just improving performance, you're cultivating a sense of belonging and shared purpose that drives collaboration, accountability, and extraordinary results.

Purpose-Driven Leadership

Today's leaders are expected to promote purpose-driven goals that align with broader societal values. Beyond financial success, leaders need to define and communicate a clear organizational purpose that resonates with their teams.

Being inclusive in discussing important societal issues will ensure the organization's purpose remains relevant and impactful.

Here's how to integrate purpose-driven leadership into your everyday practices:

Clarify Your Purpose: Start by clearly defining your organization's purpose. This should reflect not just what the company does, but why it exists and how it contributes to society. Make sure that your purpose is aligned with values that resonate with your team, customers, and broader societal goals.

Leadership Basics

Connect the Dots: Regularly connect your team's work to the larger purpose. Help them see how their individual roles contribute to the greater mission. When people understand the "why" behind their tasks, they are more motivated to contribute meaningfully.

Incorporate Societal Values: Be open and inclusive in discussions about broader societal issues that matter to your team and the community. Encourage conversations around ethics, social responsibility, and environmental sustainability, and show how these values are incorporated into your organization's purpose.

Lead by Example: As a leader, your actions should reflect the values you promote. Show commitment to purpose-driven goals by making decisions that align with those values, even if it means making difficult choices. People will follow your example and be more engaged when they see consistency between your words and actions.

Create a Culture of Purpose: Encourage your team to live the organizational purpose in their everyday work. Celebrate purpose-driven achievements, whether they're related to innovation, community involvement, or sustainability efforts. When people feel like they're part of something bigger than themselves, they'll be more committed and loyal.

Communicate Regularly: Make the organization's purpose a regular part of your communication. Whether it's through meetings, newsletters, or casual conversations, keep the purpose front and center. This reinforces alignment and reminds everyone why they're working toward the same goals.

Adapt and Evolve: Understand that societal values and priorities may shift over time. Stay attuned to these changes and be willing to adjust your organizational purpose to remain relevant and impactful. Continuous reflection and adaptation will keep your mission fresh and inspiring.

By leading with a clear, purpose-driven vision, you not only build a strong organizational culture but also inspire your team to do work that feels meaningful and connected to a greater cause.

Conclusion

As we look ahead, leadership is no longer confined to traditional practices. The trends shaping the future require leaders to be adaptable, forward-thinking, and deeply connected to the evolving needs of their teams, customers, and society. Digital transformation, remote work, DEI initiatives, sustainability, and the emphasis on soft skills are all redefining what it means to lead effectively in today's world.

To succeed in this new era, leaders must blend technical acumen with emotional intelligence, balancing innovation with responsibility. They must create environments where diverse perspectives are valued, where teams are

Leadership Basics

empowered to take ownership, and where the purpose of the organization resonates deeply with both employees and customers. Embracing continuous learning, fostering resilience, and maintaining agility in the face of rapid change will allow leaders to stay ahead of the curve and navigate the complexities of the modern workplace.

The future of leadership lies in the ability to drive meaningful change while staying true to core values. By treating team members as partners, embracing technological advancements, and promoting inclusive and sustainable practices, today's leaders will not only lead successful organizations but also inspire lasting positive impact.

Conclusion: Reflecting on Key Themes and Final Thoughts

As we reach the end of this exploration into leadership, it's essential to reflect on the key lessons and insights that have shaped our understanding of effective leadership.

Leadership is not a one-size-fits-all concept, it's a dynamic journey that evolves as we adapt to new challenges, learn from our experiences, and continuously grow both personally and professionally.

This chapter revisits the foundational themes of leadership, from the balance of theory and practice to the power of emotional intelligence and lifelong learning.

Whether you're a seasoned leader or just beginning your leadership journey, these principles serve as a guide to navigating the complexities of leadership with confidence, empathy, and resilience.

Let's look back at the core lessons, and with that reflection, be inspired to move forward with purpose and intention as we continue to grow into the leaders we are meant to be.

Leadership Basics

The Balance of Theory and Practice

Traditional leadership theories serve as a solid foundation, yet they can often fall short in real-world scenarios where unpredictability and complexity prevail.

To be effective, leaders must blend theoretical knowledge with practical experience and intuition. The ability to navigate uncertainty and adapt to changing circumstances is a hallmark of successful leadership.

Navigating Human Behavior

People's actions are often unpredictable, shaped by biases, irrational behavior, and social influences. Concepts from behavioral economics, such as loss aversion and social norms, offer leaders valuable insights into managing these challenges.

Understanding these principles helps leaders make informed decisions that account for human nature and emotional responses.

The Power of Emotional Intelligence (EI)

EI is essential for effective leadership. By developing self-awareness, self-regulation, empathy, and social skills, leaders can forge deeper connections with their teams, inspire trust, and motivate them toward success.

Jon Doolen

Leadership Basics

Leaders who are emotionally intelligent can manage their emotions, understand the emotions of others, and create a positive work environment.

Embracing Adaptive Leadership

Adaptive leadership is all about flexibility and responsiveness. It encourages leaders to embrace change, learn from failure, and foster innovation.

Unlike traditional models that focus on stability and control, adaptive leadership emphasizes the need for leaders to adjust strategies in response to shifting circumstances and evolving challenges.

Communication: The Cornerstone of Leadership

Communication is at the heart of leadership. Active listening, providing constructive feedback, and handling difficult conversations with empathy are vital for leaders. Effective communication builds trust, resolves conflicts, and aligns teams toward common goals, enabling leaders to guide their teams through challenges with clarity and confidence.

Building and Maintaining Trust

Trust is fundamental to leadership success. Leaders must be transparent, consistent, and act with integrity to build credibility with their teams, stakeholders, and clients.

Leadership Basics

Trust fosters a culture of openness and respect, which is crucial for collaboration, innovation, and long-term success.

The Power of Diversity and Inclusion

Diverse teams bring creativity, fresh perspectives, and innovative solutions.

Leaders must navigate the challenges of fostering diversity and inclusion by respecting differences of all types, promoting equitable opportunities, and leveraging the strengths of all team members.

Embracing diversity creates stronger, more effective teams capable of tackling complex problems.

Managing Conflict with Empathy and Fairness

Conflict is inevitable, but it doesn't have to disrupt team harmony. Leaders who approach conflict with empathy and fairness can resolve issues constructively, maintaining team cohesion and productivity.

Negotiation skills, along with a willingness to listen and understand different viewpoints, are key to finding solutions that benefit everyone.

The Importance of Lifelong Learning

Effective leadership requires ongoing personal development. Lifelong learning ensures that leaders remain relevant, adaptable, and capable of tackling emerging challenges.

Creating a personal development plan, seeking mentorship, and staying updated on industry trends are all crucial components of a leader's growth journey.

Navigating Change and Crisis with Resilience.

Leadership is often tested in times of change and crisis. During these moments, maintaining morale, communicating effectively, and making decisive yet empathetic decisions are essential.

Resilience allows leaders to navigate uncertainty, keeping their teams focused and motivated despite setbacks.

Final Thoughts and Encouragement

Leadership is not a destination but a journey. A journey of continuous learning, adaptation, and personal growth.

No single approach fits all situations. Flexibility, empathy, and a willingness to learn from both successes and failures are the keys to becoming an effective leader.

Authenticity is Key: Be true to your values and lead with integrity, especially when facing tough decisions. Authenticity builds trust, and when people trust you, they will follow your lead.

Leadership Basics

Embrace Change: Change is inevitable, but it's also an opportunity for growth and innovation. Stay agile, keep an open mind, and be ready to adapt when the situation demands it.

Empower Your Team: Your team is your greatest asset. Invest in their development, listen to their ideas, and create an environment where they feel valued and empowered to contribute their best.

Maintain a Positive Outlook: Leadership can be challenging, but resilience will help you overcome obstacles. Stay positive, manage stress effectively, and bounce back from setbacks with determination.

Never Stop Learning: The best leaders are committed to lifelong learning. Seek out new knowledge, skills, and experiences that will enhance your leadership capabilities. Surround yourself with mentors and peers who inspire and challenge you to grow.

Lead with Empathy: Understanding and empathizing with others fosters strong relationships and a supportive work environment. Practice active listening, show compassion, and prioritize the well-being of your team. The journey of leadership is filled with opportunities for growth, learning, and making a positive impact.

You've seen that leadership isn't a static destination but an evolving process. And that process requires ongoing effort, resilience, and commitment.

Jon Doolen

Leadership Basics

As you move forward in your leadership journey, remember that **adaptability, empathy**, and **lifelong learning** are not just nice-to-have traits, they are essential.

They are what will help you thrive in an ever-changing environment, face challenges head-on, and build teams that are not just effective but resilient.

Leadership isn't about knowing everything, it's about **being open to learning, embracing feedback**, and **growing** alongside your team. It's about creating an environment where people feel empowered to contribute their best, and where your influence helps them succeed as much as it drives the organization's success.

I invite you to continue your leadership development journey with the support and tools I offer on my website, getdoolen.com

Through my platform, I provide **affordable virtual mentorship** that can guide you through the complexities of leadership with personalized strategies.

If you're looking for guidance, actionable tools, or just a conversation about your leadership path, **I am not hard to find**.

Remember, leadership is about **people**, and you have the power to inspire, empower, and guide others. So, keep learning, stay adaptable, and always lead with integrity.

Jon Doolen

Leadership Basics

The future is in your hands, and I believe you can shape it in meaningful ways.

Thank you for taking the time to read this book, and I look forward to supporting you on your leadership journey.

Jon Doolen

Leadership Basics

Citations

(Citation 1)

Trait Theory was primarily developed through the work of several psychologists who sought to understand and categorize personality traits. Some of the key contributors to the development of Trait Theory include:

1. **Gordon Allport:**
    - Often considered the founder of Trait Theory, Allport introduced the idea that personality is made up of stable and enduring traits. He categorized traits into three levels:
        - **Cardinal Traits:** Dominate an individual's entire personality.
        - **Central Traits:** Found in most people and define personality.
        - **Secondary Traits:** More situation-specific and less consistent.
2. **Raymond Cattell:**
    - Built on Allport's work and used statistical methods like factor analysis to identify core traits.
    - He developed the **16 Personality Factor (16PF) Model**, which describes 16 primary personality traits.
3. **Hans Eysenck:**
    - Focused on identifying broader dimensions of personality traits.
    - Proposed a model with three major traits: **Extraversion-Introversion, Neuroticism-**

Leadership Basics

Emotional Stability, and later added **Psychoticism**.
4. **The Big Five Personality Traits**:
   - Developed through the collaborative work of many researchers, particularly Paul Costa and Robert McCrae.
   - This model identifies five broad dimensions of personality: **Openness**, **Conscientiousness**, **Extraversion**, **Agreeableness**, and **Neuroticism** (OCEAN).

Trait Theory has evolved over time, with contributions from various psychologists refining its focus and application in understanding personality.

(Citation 2)

The **Behavioral Theory of Leadership** was developed through the research efforts of multiple psychologists and scholars during the mid-20th century. The focus shifted from innate traits to observable behaviors of effective leaders. Key contributors include:

1. The Ohio State University Studies
- **Researchers**: Ralph Stogdill and others.
- **Contribution**: Identified two main leadership behaviors:
  - **Initiating Structure**: Task-oriented behaviors focused on organizing work and achieving goals.
  - **Consideration**: People-oriented behaviors focused on building trust and relationships.

2. The University of Michigan Studies
- **Researchers**: Rensis Likert and his team.
- **Contribution**: Distinguished between:
    - **Task-oriented leaders**: Focused on productivity and efficiency.
    - **Employee-oriented leaders**: Focused on the well-being and development of team members.

3. Kurt Lewin and the Iowa Studies
- **Researchers**: Kurt Lewin, Ronald Lippitt, and Ralph White.
- **Contribution**: Identified three primary leadership styles:
    - **Authoritarian (Autocratic)**
    - **Democratic**
    - **Laissez-faire**

4. Blake and Mouton's Managerial Grid
- **Developers**: Robert Blake and Jane Mouton.
- **Contribution**: Created a grid plotting leadership behaviors on two axes:
    - Concern for People.
    - Concern for Production.
- Resulted in five leadership styles, including the "Team Leader" as the most effective.

These foundational studies contributed significantly to the understanding of leadership behaviors, forming the basis for modern leadership training and development practices.

Leadership Basics

(Citation 3)

The **Contingency Theory of Leadership** was primarily developed by **Fred Fiedler**, a prominent psychologist and researcher. His work emphasized that there is no single best way to lead; instead, the effectiveness of a leader depends on the alignment between their leadership style and the situation.

Key Contributions:
1. **Fiedler's Contingency Model**:
    - Proposed in the 1960s.
    - Fiedler identified two primary leadership styles:
        - **Task-Oriented Leaders**: Focus on achieving goals and completing tasks.
        - **Relationship-Oriented Leaders**: Focus on building strong relationships and team cohesion.
    - Introduced the **Least Preferred Co-Worker (LPC) scale** to determine a leader's style.
    - Effectiveness depends on the **situational favorableness**, determined by:
1. **Leader-Member Relations**: The level of trust and respect between the leader and team.
2. **Task Structure**: The clarity and organization of tasks.
3. **Position Power**: The leader's authority within the organization.
    2. **Other Contributors**:
        - **Hersey and Blanchard**: Developed the **Situational Leadership Theory**, which is

closely related to contingency theories and emphasizes adaptability based on team readiness and maturity.
- **Path-Goal Theory** (by Robert House): Another contingency-based model that focuses on how leaders can adjust their behavior to help followers achieve their goals.

Fiedler's work laid the foundation for understanding that leadership effectiveness is context-dependent, influencing modern leadership development and training.

(Citation 4)

Transformational Leadership Theory is a framework that explains how leaders can inspire and motivate followers to achieve extraordinary results by transforming their attitudes, behaviors, and expectations. It was first introduced by **James MacGregor Burns** in 1978 and further developed by **Bernard Bass** in the 1980s.

Core Principles of Transformational Leadership Theory
The theory outlines how leaders create significant change by focusing on the following:
1. **Creating a Vision:**
    - Leaders provide a clear and compelling vision of the future that motivates followers to work toward shared goals.
2. **Inspiring and Motivating Followers:**
    - By appealing to emotions and values, leaders encourage commitment and enthusiasm.
3. **Challenging the Status Quo:**

Leadership Basics

- - Leaders foster creativity and innovation, urging followers to think critically and solve problems in new ways.
  4. **Building Trust and Relationships**:
     - Leaders act as role models, gaining respect and trust through their actions and integrity.
  5. **Developing Followers**:
     - Leaders focus on the growth and personal development of their followers, mentoring and coaching them to reach their potential.

Four Components of Transformational Leadership
Bernard Bass expanded the theory by identifying four key behaviors of transformational leaders, often referred to as the "4 I's":
1. **Idealized Influence**:
   - Leaders serve as role models, demonstrating high ethical standards and earning admiration and trust.
2. **Inspirational Motivation**:
   - Leaders articulate an inspiring vision and use enthusiasm to motivate followers.
3. **Intellectual Stimulation**:
   - Leaders encourage creativity, innovation, and critical thinking, challenging followers to solve problems.
4. **Individualized Consideration**:
   - Leaders provide personalized support, recognizing individual needs and helping followers grow.

Leadership Basics

Benefits of Transformational Leadership Theory
- Encourages high levels of **motivation** and **engagement** among followers.
- Promotes **innovation** and **problem-solving**.
- Strengthens **team dynamics** and organizational culture.
- Leads to greater **organizational change** and adaptability.

Criticism of the Theory
- May rely too heavily on the charisma or personal influence of the leader.
- Difficult to implement in highly structured or bureaucratic environments.
- Requires significant effort to balance individualized attention with broader organizational needs.

Applications of Transformational Leadership Theory
- **In Business**: Driving change, inspiring innovation, and improving employee engagement.
- **In Education**: Inspiring students and educators to achieve higher levels of performance.
- **In Social Movements**: Leaders like Martin Luther King Jr. embody transformational leadership by inspiring societal change.

(Citation 5)

Servant Leadership Theory is a leadership philosophy that prioritizes the needs of others, especially team members and the community, over the self-interest of the leader. The

Leadership Basics

leader's primary goal is to serve, empower, and develop others, creating an environment where people can thrive and perform at their best.

The concept was introduced by **Robert K. Greenleaf** in his 1970 essay, *The Servant as Leader*. Greenleaf argued that the most effective leaders are those who focus on serving first and leading second.

Key Principles of Servant Leadership
Greenleaf outlined several characteristics that define servant leaders:
1. **Listening:**
    - Actively listening to understand the needs, concerns, and ideas of others.
    - Example: A leader who prioritizes one-on-one meetings to hear employee feedback.
2. **Empathy:**
    - Understanding and sharing the feelings of team members.
    - Example: Recognizing and addressing the struggles of employees in challenging times.
3. **Healing:**
    - Helping others recover emotionally and grow, fostering a positive environment.
    - Example: Supporting team members during conflicts or personal hardships.
4. **Awareness:**
    - Being self-aware and understanding the impact of one's actions on others.

Leadership Basics

- Example: A leader who reflects on their decisions to ensure they align with the team's well-being.
5. **Persuasion:**
    - Influencing others through reason and collaboration rather than authority.
    - Example: Building consensus rather than issuing orders.
6. **Conceptualization:**
    - Seeing the bigger picture and creating a vision for the future.
    - Example: Setting long-term goals while managing day-to-day tasks effectively.
7. **Foresight:**
    - Anticipating the consequences of decisions and preparing for the future.
    - Example: Identifying potential challenges before they arise.
8. **Stewardship:**
    - Taking responsibility for the well-being of the organization and its people.
    - Example: Ensuring resources are used responsibly to benefit everyone.
9. **Commitment to the Growth of People:**
    - Supporting the personal and professional development of team members.
    - Example: Providing training, mentorship, and career development opportunities.
10. **Building Community:**
    - Fostering a sense of belonging and collaboration.

Leadership Basics

- o Example: Encouraging team bonding and creating a culture of mutual support.

Key Focus of Servant Leadership
- **Others First**: Serving others' needs before personal or organizational goals.
- **Empowerment**: Helping team members grow, succeed, and reach their full potential.
- **Ethical Leadership**: Acting with integrity and making morally sound decisions.
- **Long-Term Impact**: Building lasting relationships and sustainable practices.

Benefits of Servant Leadership
- Increased **trust** and **engagement** among employees.
- Improved **team morale** and collaboration.
- Encourages **innovation** by empowering individuals to share ideas.
- Fosters a positive and people-centered organizational culture.

Criticism of Servant Leadership
- May be seen as too "soft" or idealistic in highly competitive environments.
- Can be challenging to balance servant leadership with achieving organizational goals.
- Requires leaders to possess a high level of emotional intelligence and patience.

Leadership Basics

Examples of Servant Leaders
- **Mahatma Gandhi**: Focused on serving and empowering the Indian people during the fight for independence.
- **Mother Teresa**: Dedicated her life to serving the poor and vulnerable.
- **Herb Kelleher (Southwest Airlines)**: Fostered an employee-first culture to drive company success.

(Citation 6)

The concept of **Contextual Intelligence** was first documented and popularized by **Robert J. Sternberg**, an American psychologist, in his framework for "Successful Intelligence." Sternberg introduced contextual intelligence as one of the three types of intelligence in his **Triarchic Theory of Intelligence** (the other two being analytical intelligence and creative intelligence).

Sternberg described contextual intelligence as the ability to adapt to, shape, and select environments to achieve goals. It emphasizes practical problem-solving and the ability to assess and respond to the nuances of different social, cultural, and situational contexts.

Later, the term gained traction in leadership studies, particularly through the work of **Tarun Khanna**, a professor at Harvard Business School, who explored contextual intelligence in the global business landscape. Khanna applied the concept to understanding and adapting

Leadership Basics

strategies to different cultural and regional business contexts.

(Citation 7)

Behavioral economics is primarily credited to two influential scholars: **Daniel Kahneman** and **Amos Tversky**. Their groundbreaking work in the 1970s and 1980s on cognitive biases and decision-making laid the foundation for this field. They demonstrated how human behavior often deviates from the purely rational models assumed in classical economics.
Key contributions include:
1. **Daniel Kahneman** - His book *Thinking, Fast and Slow* popularized behavioral economics concepts like *System 1 and System 2 thinking* (intuitive vs. deliberate thought processes). Kahneman was awarded the **Nobel Prize in Economic Sciences in 2002**, though Tversky was not eligible due to his passing in 1996.
2. **Amos Tversky** - Together with Kahneman, Tversky developed *Prospect Theory*, which explains how people perceive gains and losses differently, leading to irrational financial and decision-making behavior.

Other significant contributors to behavioral economics include:
- **Richard Thaler**, who expanded the field by applying behavioral insights to real-world scenarios like savings, investment, and policy-making. His book *Nudge* (co-authored with Cass Sunstein) introduced the concept of "nudging" to encourage better

decision-making. Thaler received the **Nobel Prize in Economic Sciences in 2017**.
- **Herbert Simon**, an earlier pioneer, introduced the concept of "bounded rationality," which influenced the development of behavioral economics by highlighting the limits of human rationality in decision-making.

These scholars collectively shaped the modern understanding of how psychological factors influence economic behavior.

(Citation 8)

Traditional Economic Theory in Leadership does not have a single founder but rather evolves from the broader field of **classical economics**, which was primarily developed by early economists like **Adam Smith, David Ricardo**, and **John Stuart Mill**.

These thinkers laid the foundation for understanding decision-making, resource allocation, and productivity, which influenced leadership concepts based on rationality and efficiency.

Key Figures Associated with Traditional Economic Theory in Leadership:
1. **Adam Smith** (1723–1790):
    - Often called the "Father of Economics," Smith's work, particularly *The Wealth of Nations*, introduced the concept of the *invisible hand*, emphasizing rational decision-

making and self-interest as drivers of economic efficiency. These ideas influenced early leadership models focused on productivity and profit maximization.
2. **Frederick Winslow Taylor** (1856–1915):
    - Known as the father of **Scientific Management**, Taylor applied economic principles to organizational leadership and operations. He believed in breaking down tasks for maximum efficiency, rational decision-making, and incentivizing workers through monetary rewards. His ideas shaped early leadership practices in industrial settings.
3. **Max Weber** (1864–1920):
    - Weber's work on **bureaucratic management** is rooted in rational-legal authority, emphasizing structured hierarchies, clear rules, and objective decision-making. This aligns with traditional economic assumptions of predictability and efficiency in leadership.
4. **Herbert Simon** (1916–2001):
    - While Simon is better known for his work on **bounded rationality**, his earlier contributions to decision theory were grounded in traditional economic assumptions of rational choice, influencing leadership models based on logical and systematic decision-making.

Leadership Basics

Influence on Leadership:
Traditional Economic Theory in Leadership reflects the economic models of these figures, focusing on rational decision-making, profit maximization, and efficiency. Over time, this approach has been critiqued and expanded with insights from psychology, sociology, and behavioral economics, leading to more human-centered leadership models.

(Citation 9)

Confirmation Bias—the tendency to seek, interpret, and remember information that confirms one's existing beliefs—is primarily credited to the work of **Peter Wason**, a British cognitive psychologist.
Key Contributions:
1. **Peter Wason** (1924–2003):
   - Wason first documented confirmation bias in the 1960s through his **Wason Selection Task**, a logical reasoning experiment. He demonstrated that people tend to favor information that supports their preconceptions while ignoring contradictory evidence.
2. **Amos Tversky and Daniel Kahneman**:
   - While not the originators of the term, Tversky and Kahneman expanded on confirmation bias in their work on cognitive biases and heuristics, showing how it impacts decision-making and judgment under uncertainty. Their research further solidified confirmation bias

as a central concept in behavioral economics and psychology.
3. **Francis Bacon** (Historical Influence):
    - Long before modern psychology, Francis Bacon (1561–1626) hinted at the idea of confirmation bias in his work *Novum Organum*. He described how people tend to focus on evidence that supports their beliefs while ignoring contrary evidence, though he did not use the modern term.

(Citation 10)

Anchoring Bias, the cognitive bias where people rely too heavily on the first piece of information (the "anchor") when making decisions, is primarily credited to the groundbreaking work of **Amos Tversky** and **Daniel Kahneman**.

Key Contributions:
1. **Amos Tversky and Daniel Kahneman**:
    - They first documented **anchoring bias** in their seminal paper *Judgment under Uncertainty: Heuristics and Biases* (1974). In their experiments, they showed how individuals make estimates by starting with an initial value (the anchor) and adjusting insufficiently, leading to biased outcomes.
    - For example, they demonstrated how people estimating numbers (like percentages or quantities) were influenced by irrelevant

anchors presented during the task, even when they knew the anchors were arbitrary.
2. **Experimental Example**:
    - In one experiment, participants were asked if the percentage of African countries in the United Nations was higher or lower than a random number spun on a wheel. Their subsequent estimates were biased toward the number they had seen, even though it was unrelated.

Broader Impact:

The concept of anchoring bias has since been widely applied across fields, including **behavioral economics**, **marketing**, **negotiation strategies**, and **financial decision-making**. Tversky and Kahneman's work in this area earned Kahneman the **Nobel Prize in Economic Sciences in 2002**, as it formed a cornerstone of behavioral economics and the understanding of human judgment and decision-making.

(Citation 11)

The **Availability Heuristic**, a cognitive shortcut where people estimate the likelihood of events based on how easily examples come to mind, is credited to **Amos Tversky** and **Daniel Kahneman**.
Key Contributions:
1. **Amos Tversky and Daniel Kahneman**:
    - They introduced the concept in their seminal 1973 paper *Availability: A Heuristic for Judging*

> *Frequency and Probability*. They demonstrated that people rely on the ease of recalling instances when estimating probabilities, leading to biases in judgment.
>   - For example, if someone recently heard about airplane crashes, they might overestimate the frequency of such events, despite their rarity, because those examples are more readily "available" in memory.

Notable Findings:
- The availability heuristic explains why **recent events** or **emotionally charged events** disproportionately influence people's perceptions of risk or probability.
- It also sheds light on why people may fear rare but dramatic events (like shark attacks) more than common but less sensational risks (like car accidents).

Broader Impact:

The concept has been widely applied in fields like **behavioral economics, risk assessment**, and **decision-making**, showing how mental shortcuts can lead to systematic errors in judgment. Tversky and Kahneman's work on this and other heuristics played a foundational role in the development of **behavioral science**, ultimately earning Kahneman the **Nobel Prize in Economic Sciences in 2002**.

Leadership Basics

(Citation 12)

Emotional Intelligence (EI) is primarily credited to **Daniel Goleman**, an American psychologist and author, who popularized the concept in his 1995 best-selling book, *Emotional Intelligence: Why It Can Matter More Than IQ*. However, the foundational work was laid by earlier researchers.

Key Contributors:
1. **Peter Salovey and John D. Mayer:**
    - Salovey and Mayer, psychologists, introduced the term *Emotional Intelligence* in 1990. They defined it as the ability to perceive, understand, regulate, and use emotions to facilitate thought and action.
    - Their work focused on understanding how emotional skills impact social interactions, problem-solving, and personal well-being.
2. **Daniel Goleman:**
    - Goleman expanded on Salovey and Mayer's research and made it accessible to a broader audience. He emphasized how emotional intelligence affects leadership, relationships, and workplace success, identifying key components like:
        - **Self-awareness**
        - **Self-regulation**
        - **Motivation**
        - **Empathy**
        - **Social skills**

3. **Howard Gardner:**
    - While not directly associated with EI, Gardner's **Theory of Multiple Intelligences** (1983) introduced the idea of **interpersonal intelligence** and **intrapersonal intelligence**, which align closely with concepts of emotional intelligence.

Summary:
- **Peter Salovey and John Mayer** are credited with formally defining emotional intelligence in academic research.
- **Daniel Goleman** is credited with popularizing the concept and demonstrating its importance in personal and professional success.

(Citation 13)

The term **Emotional Quotient (EQ)** is often associated with **Daniel Goleman**, as he popularized the concept of **Emotional Intelligence (EI)** in the 1990s. However, the origins of measuring emotional abilities and relating them to intelligence predate Goleman.

Key Contributors to Emotional Quotient:
1. **Reuven Bar-On:**
    - Psychologist **Reuven Bar-On** is credited with coining the term *Emotional Quotient (EQ)* in the 1980s.
    - He developed the **Bar-On Emotional Quotient Inventory (EQ-i)**, one of the first tools to measure emotional intelligence. His work focused on emotional and social

Leadership Basics

> functioning as key contributors to success in life.
2. **Peter Salovey and John Mayer**:
   - While they didn't use the term *EQ*, they are foundational figures in the study of **Emotional Intelligence (EI)** and its components, as they introduced the concept in 1990. Their work laid the groundwork for assessing and understanding emotional skills.
3. **Daniel Goleman**:
   - Although Goleman did not originate the term *EQ*, his 1995 book *Emotional Intelligence: Why It Can Matter More Than IQ* brought global attention to emotional intelligence and how it could be as important—or more important—than cognitive intelligence (IQ).

Summary:
- **Reuven Bar-On** is directly credited with coining and developing *Emotional Quotient (EQ)* as a measurable concept.
- **Peter Salovey and John Mayer** laid the academic foundation for the broader concept of emotional intelligence.
- **Daniel Goleman** popularized the concept, making EQ a mainstream topic in leadership, workplace dynamics, and personal development.

(Citation 14)

Adaptive Leadership is primarily credited to **Ronald Heifetz**, a professor at Harvard University, along with his

Leadership Basics

colleagues **Marty Linsky** and later **Alexander Grashow**. The concept was introduced and developed through their work at the Harvard Kennedy School and their books on leadership.

Key Contributions:

1. **Ronald Heifetz**:
    - Heifetz first introduced the concept in his 1994 book *Leadership Without Easy Answers*. He defined Adaptive Leadership as the practice of mobilizing people to tackle tough challenges and thrive in changing environments.
    - He emphasized the distinction between **technical challenges** (solvable with expertise and existing knowledge) and **adaptive challenges** (requiring changes in beliefs, values, or behaviors).
2. **Marty Linsky**:
    - Co-authored *Leadership on the Line* (2002) with Heifetz. Together, they expanded on the concept, providing practical tools for leaders to navigate adaptive challenges and manage resistance to change.
3. **Alexander Grashow**:
    - Co-authored *The Practice of Adaptive Leadership* (2009) with Heifetz and Linsky. This work introduced a hands-on approach to applying adaptive leadership principles in organizations and communities.

Leadership Basics

Ronald Heifetz is the primary originator of Adaptive Leadership, supported and expanded by **Marty Linsky** and **Alexander Grashow**. Their work is foundational in modern leadership studies, especially in guiding organizations and leaders through complex, evolving challenges.

(Citation 15)

Autocratic Leadership theory, a style where the leader makes decisions unilaterally and expects obedience from subordinates, is not attributed to a single individual in the way some leadership theories are. However, it emerged as a concept within the broader study of leadership styles, particularly in the early to mid-20th century.
Key Contributors and Historical Development:
1. **Kurt Lewin** (1930s):
    - **Kurt Lewin**, a pioneering social psychologist, is one of the earliest researchers credited with formally identifying and categorizing leadership styles, including **autocratic leadership,** as part of his study on leadership behaviors in the 1930s.
    - In an influential study, Lewin and his colleagues identified three main leadership styles: **autocratic, democratic,** and **laissez-faire.**
        - **Autocratic leaders** make decisions independently, without consulting others, and expect compliance.
        - This study provided empirical support for the idea that leadership styles

Leadership Basics

   influence group dynamics and productivity.
2. **Douglas McGregor** (1960s):
   - McGregor, in his work on management theory, particularly with his concepts of **Theory X** and **Theory Y**, expanded on the autocratic style.
     - **Theory X** assumes that employees are inherently lazy, need to be controlled, and must be directed (which aligns with autocratic leadership).
     - While McGregor didn't explicitly create the autocratic leadership theory, his framework helped shape thinking about leadership and management styles in a more structured way.
3. **Max Weber** (Early 20th Century):
   - **Max Weber**, a sociologist, explored the concept of **bureaucratic leadership**, which shares some similarities with autocratic leadership, particularly in its emphasis on hierarchy and strict rules. While Weber didn't directly coin the term "autocratic leadership," his work on authority structures and leadership within organizations influenced the development of leadership theories, including autocracy.

Summary:
- **Kurt Lewin** is credited with pioneering the formal identification of autocratic leadership as a distinct leadership style in the 1930s.

Leadership Basics

- **Douglas McGregor** and **Max Weber** contributed indirectly to the development and understanding of autocratic leadership through their work on management theory and authority structures.

Autocratic leadership remains a topic of study within leadership theory, often discussed in contrast to more democratic or participatory leadership styles.

(Citation 16)

Democratic Leadership theory, also known as **Participative Leadership**, is largely credited to **Kurt Lewin**, the same social psychologist who helped develop the foundational concepts of leadership styles, including autocratic and laissez-faire leadership, in the 1930s.
Key Contributors and Historical Development:
1. **Kurt Lewin** (1930s):
    - **Kurt Lewin** is widely regarded as the first to formalize the concept of **Democratic Leadership**. In his famous leadership study in the 1930s, Lewin and his colleagues identified three primary leadership styles: **autocratic**, **democratic**, and **laissez-faire**.
        - **Democratic leaders** encourage participation and input from their team members, and decisions are made collaboratively. This style promotes open communication, shared decision-making, and a more inclusive approach to leadership.

Leadership Basics

- Lewin's research showed that democratic leadership generally led to higher satisfaction and motivation among group members, as it allowed for more engagement and autonomy in the decision-making process.

2. **Douglas McGregor** (1960s):
    - While **McGregor** didn't directly create **Democratic Leadership** theory, his **Theory Y** concept significantly aligns with democratic leadership principles. **Theory Y** assumes that people are motivated, self-directed, and capable of making decisions on their own, which is a core idea behind democratic leadership.
    - McGregor's work helped reinforce the idea that employees are more productive and innovative when they are given a voice in decision-making and when their input is valued.

3. **Ralph Stogdill** (1974):
    - **Ralph Stogdill** contributed to leadership theory with his work on leadership traits, styles, and group dynamics, further validating the benefits of democratic leadership in terms of group effectiveness and member satisfaction.

Summary:
- **Kurt Lewin** is credited with formally identifying and categorizing **Democratic Leadership** in the 1930s as part of his pioneering work on leadership styles.

- **Douglas McGregor's** Theory Y further supported the democratic leadership approach, emphasizing collaboration, trust, and empowerment of team members.
- **Ralph Stogdill** also contributed to reinforcing the value of democratic leadership, particularly in promoting group cohesion and productivity.

Democratic leadership emphasizes shared decision-making, collaboration, and an inclusive approach, typically leading to higher morale, creativity, and engagement in teams.

(Citation 17)

Laissez-faire Leadership style, characterized by a hands-off approach where leaders give employees a high degree of autonomy and decision-making power, is primarily credited to **Kurt Lewin** as part of his leadership styles research in the 1930s. However, several other researchers have contributed to its development and understanding over time.

Key Contributors:

1. **Kurt Lewin** (1930s):
    - **Kurt Lewin**, a pioneering social psychologist, is often credited with formally identifying the **laissez-faire leadership style** in his 1939 research, which categorized leadership into three primary styles: **autocratic, democratic,** and **laissez-faire.**
    - In Lewin's study, **laissez-faire leadership** was defined by leaders who allow team members to make decisions with little to no

Leadership Basics

     interference, often leaving them to set their own goals and work at their own pace.
   - His studies found that laissez-faire leadership often led to low levels of productivity and cohesiveness among the group but could be effective in situations where team members were highly skilled and self-motivated.
2. **Douglas McGregor** (1960s):
   - While **Douglas McGregor** did not specifically coin **laissez-faire leadership**, his **Theory X and Theory Y** helped provide a framework for understanding when laissez-faire might be effective.
     - **Theory Y** supports a more relaxed, hands-off leadership style by assuming that employees are self-motivated and capable of making decisions independently, which aligns with laissez-faire leadership principles.
3. **Ralph Stogdill** (1974):
   - **Ralph Stogdill**, an influential leadership theorist, contributed to the understanding of various leadership styles, including laissez-faire. He emphasized the importance of understanding how leadership style affects group dynamics and task performance, noting that laissez-faire leadership could sometimes be ineffective if group members lacked direction or needed more guidance.

Summary:

Jon Doolen

Leadership Basics

- **Kurt Lewin** is credited with first identifying and categorizing **laissez-faire leadership** as one of three main leadership styles in his 1939 research.
- **Douglas McGregor** and **Ralph Stogdill** further contributed to the understanding of laissez-faire leadership by exploring its role in the context of employee autonomy, motivation, and group dynamics.

Laissez-faire leadership is often seen as most effective when team members are highly skilled, experienced, and self-directed, but it can be problematic in situations where more direction and supervision are needed.

(Citation 18)

The **Eisenhower Matrix**, also known as the **Eisenhower Decision Matrix** or the **Urgent-Important Matrix**, is credited to **Dwight D. Eisenhower**, the 34th President of the United States and a five-star general in the U.S. Army. The matrix is a tool for prioritizing tasks based on their urgency and importance, helping individuals focus on what truly matters.
Key Contributor:
- **Dwight D. Eisenhower:**
    - Eisenhower famously said, "What is important is seldom urgent and what is urgent is seldom important." This idea led to the creation of the matrix, which helps people distinguish between tasks that require immediate attention and those that are important but not necessarily urgent.

Jon Doolen

Leadership Basics

> o Although Eisenhower did not formally develop the matrix as we know it today, his leadership and time-management practices inspired the framework. He applied this concept to manage his time effectively, balancing his responsibilities as a general and president.

The Eisenhower Matrix:
The matrix divides tasks into four quadrants based on two criteria:
1. **Important and Urgent (Do):** Tasks that require immediate attention, such as crises or pressing deadlines.
2. **Important but Not Urgent (Plan):** Tasks that are significant but don't need to be done immediately, like long-term projects or personal development.
3. **Not Important but Urgent (Delegate):** Tasks that need to be addressed soon but do not significantly contribute to your goals, like interruptions or some meetings.
4. **Not Important and Not Urgent (Eliminate):** Tasks that are neither urgent nor important, such as trivial distractions.

Summary:
- **Dwight D. Eisenhower** is credited with the concept behind the **Eisenhower Matrix**, although the formalized tool and its widespread usage have evolved over time.
- The matrix is a highly effective time-management tool for prioritizing tasks based on their urgency and

Leadership Basics

> importance, helping people focus on what truly contributes to their goals.

(Citation 19)

The **Pomodoro Technique** is credited to **Francesco Cirillo**, an Italian entrepreneur and developer. He created the technique in the late 1980s as a way to improve personal productivity and time management.

Key Contributor:
- **Francesco Cirillo:**
    - Cirillo developed the Pomodoro Technique when he was a university student. The method uses a timer (often a kitchen timer shaped like a tomato, or *"pomodoro"* in Italian) to break work into intervals, typically 25 minutes in length, separated by short breaks.
    - The core idea of the technique is to enhance focus and concentration by working in short bursts with frequent breaks, helping to avoid mental fatigue and improve productivity.

How the Pomodoro Technique Works:
1. **Set a Timer:** Work for 25 minutes (one "Pomodoro").
2. **Take a Break:** After 25 minutes, take a short 5-minute break.
3. **Repeat:** After four "Pomodoros," take a longer break, typically 15–30 minutes.
4. **Track Progress:** Keep track of how many Pomodoros you complete to stay motivated and organized.

Summary:

Jon Doolen

Leadership Basics

- **Francesco Cirillo** is credited with creating the **Pomodoro Technique** in the late 1980s.
- The technique has since become widely used for time management, especially for tasks requiring intense focus or tackling large projects by breaking them down into manageable, focused intervals.

Disclaimers

This book is not an attack on previous leadership books but rather an addendum to the existing body of knowledge. I have tremendous respect for those who have come before me and those who come after me. If you have a genuine desire to help others today than they were yesterday, I am clapping for you.

These are my thoughts, opinions, and experiences. I consulted many influential leaders in my life to help shape this content. When possible, I've credited them, but if you recognize something you shared with me, feel free to reach out, and I'll ensure you get the proper credit. I don't claim to be the smartest person in the room, I'm always open to fact-checking and learning from others.

I have made mistakes. I will make more mistakes. It's ok to make mistakes as long as you learn from them. I have made some mistakes in some of the relationships I have had over the years, and if you're reading this and I have made mistake that frustrated you or cost me the benefit of your friendship, I apologize but also thank you for reading the book.

www.ingramcontent.com/pod-product-compliance
Lightning Source LLC
Chambersburg PA
CBHW050136170426
43197CB00011B/1858